T0208670

There is Always Room for One More at One More at Our Dinner Table

Volga German Stories and Recipes

Rebecca Nab Young

authorHOUSE®

AuthorHouse™
1663 Liberty Drive
Bloomington, IN 47403
www.authorhouse.com
Phone: 1-800-839-8640

First published by AuthorHouse 4/1/2011

ISBN: 978-1-4567-2892-2 (e)
ISBN: 978-1-4567-2891-5 (hc)
ISBN: 978-1-4567-2893-9 (sc)

Library of Congress Control Number: 2011900164

Printed in the United States of America

Dedication

MY SOUL WAS BORN IN RUSSIA next to the Volga River. I am not Russian, however. My ancestors came to Russia from Germany in the 1760s to homestead on land given to them by Tsarina Catherine who was also German born. Catherine had become Empress of all Russia when her husband Tsar Peter III was deposed and assassinated in 1762. She needed help taming the Russian Steppes, which were open prairie lands like our North and South Dakota. She knew her people to be hardworking and tenacious. My great, great, great, great grandfather was Wilhelm Nab, born in 1743. He was a miller from Darmstadt and arrived in the German village of Kraft, Russia in 1766.

It took my grandfather almost one year to get from Germany to Saint Petersburg on a ship named the *Elephant*, and then by wagon to Kraft. Many, many Germans died making the long trek to the Steppes. Many more died that first winter because they had no homes or crops. It was a harsh life with long winters filled with death. Only the strongest survived to flourish and establish more villages and farms. The new German homesteaders did not mingle with the Russian people much. They kept to themselves and their own ways.

My people lived in Russia for about 250 years before revolution and persecution became inevitable. When revolution arrived in 1874 and subsequent years, more began migrating; however, this time it was mostly to America. My grandparents came to America between 1901 and 1912. My mother's mother Anna Marie Bauer was only 1 year old when she arrived in America, but my father's mother Susanna Nab was thirty-one. Grandma Nab always missed her home in Russia, and she continued to speak German and dress in smocks worn over a long dress. She had very long white hair that she wore in a bun on the top of her head. She never learned to speak or write English. I never saw her in a pair of pants. Grandma Bauer, on the other hand, was modern. She wore her hair short, she wore pants, and she spoke English. My mother Helen didn't speak German until she was 18 and married my father Harold. Mom and Dad lived with his parents on their farm for over a year, so because Grandma Nab couldn't speak English, my mother learned German. My mother and father spoke German quite a lot at home when I was a child, but mother wanted us to be "real" Americans, so speaking German eventually stopped in our household. My mother is one of the last people I know who still speaks the ancient German dialect brought from Russia.

I grew up on many farms that my father rented. We grew corn, pinto beans, white beans, sugar beets, and alfalfa. Even though we were poor by today's standards, we had plenty to eat. We had three milk cows and dozens of chickens. Mom also had a big garden, and she and I spent a lot of the summer canning and freezing corn, tomatoes, peas, and so on. Mom bought lugs of apricots, peaches, pears, and cherries for us to can. We had a room in the basement where we stored jars of fruits, jellies, pickles, and vegetables. It was a wonderful sight—all the rows of food for the winter. We called this room the fruit room.

My grandmothers, mother, and aunts were all great cooks; everything was cooked from scratch from recipes handed down from the Russian villages. Each woman in the family had her own specialty and no one else would bring that dish to our family gatherings. Aunt Esther Wagner made the best grebbles or sugared doughnuts. Aunt Esther Schmidt made a delicious vegetable soup. My mother made the great cabbage buns and still does.

I wrote down my family recipes so that they will not be lost for all time. Some of the recipes I learned how to make over the years from watching my mother, grandmothers, and aunts. Some have become family favorites. This book is dedicated to all the brave Volga German women who made the journey to Russia and then to America. I especially dedicate it to my grandmothers Anna Marie Bauer and Susanna Kinsfather Nab, to my Mother Helen Bauer Nab, and to my daughter Nikki Innes Alford who asked me to write this book. I want to thank my grandmothers for all the great food and recipes and my mother for teaching me how to cook and keep the ways of Unserer Leute, which means, our people.

With my best wishes for eating well and enjoying a walk back in time.

Important Dates in the Lives of German Russians

April 21, 1729   Sophia Augusta Frederica of Anhalt-Zerbst was born in Germany. She later ruled Russia with the name of Catherine II, better known as Catherine the Great.

1756–1763   *The Seven Years' War takes place. It is an important factor in bringing Germans to the Lower Volga to establish colonies.*

June 28, 1762   *Catherine II, or Catherine the Great, ascends to the throne of Russia.*

December 4, 1762   The first Manifesto is issued by Catherine II. She invites foreigners to come to Russia to live. The invitation brings few to the country.

July 22, 1763   Catherine II issues a second manifesto. It spells out in detail the conditions under which foreigners can immigrate and grants them special privileges and rights. Large numbers of German peasants accept the invitation to live in the country.

1764–1767   *German colonies are founded along the lower Volga River.*

1771–1774   Kirghiz raids during Pugachev's rebellion in what is called the Pugachevshchina. The Volga colonies are decimated as a result.

1786   Mennonites from West Prussia begin coming to Russia because the 1772 Partition of Poland threatens military exemptions that the Mennonites make use of as conscientious objectors. The Mennonites settle primarily in the Taurida region in southern Russia.

1793	The second partition of Poland grants an area of Volhynia to Russia. Polish landowners invite the German peasants to lease land for farming.
November 6, 1796	*Catherine II dies at the age of 67.*
1796–1801	*The son of Catherine II Czar Paul I reigns.*
1801–1825	*Tsar Alexander I, the beloved grandson of Catherine II, reigns.*
February 20, 1804	*Alexander I modifies and reissues the Manifesto of Catherine II, inviting foreigners to settle in New Russia.*
1825–1855	Tsar Nicholas I, who is the grandson of Catherine II and a brother of Alexander I, reigns.
1830	A Polish insurrection brings the immigration of many Polish Germans to the Bessarabia and lower Volga region.
1855–1881	This is the time of the reign of Tsar Alexander II, great grandson of Catherine II and the son of Nicholas I.
1860s	Another flood of Germans immigrate to Volhynia prompted by the abolishment of serfdom. This leaves a significant lack of a work force. A second Polish uprising in 1862 brings more Polish Germans to Volhynia and other parts of Russia.
1871	Germany is unified as a nation for the first time. This created great unease among other European nations and Russia. It is a time of animosity toward foreigners in Russia

due to a Slavophile movement and growing nationalism.

June 4, 1871	The Imperial Russian Government issues a decree repealing the manifestos of Catherine II and Alexander I. It terminated the special privileges of the German colonists.
January 13, 1874	The Imperial Government of Russia issues a second manifesto amending the previous one. This decree institutes compulsory military conscription for the German colonists. This sends thousands of German Russians fleeing to North and South America.
1881–1917	This is the reign of Tsar Nicholas II, a descendent of Catherine II. He abdicates during World War I. On July 16, 1918, the Bolsheviks execute him and his family. Nicholas II is the last monarch to rule in Russia.
July 28, 1914	*The start of World War I.*
1915	The Eastern Front advances. The Volhynian Germans are deported to the Lower Volga and South Russia.
December 13, 1916	The Volga Germans are ordered to be banished. This is never carried out because of other troubles in Russia at that time.
November 7, 1917	The Bolshevik Revolution in Russia is led by Vlaimir Lenin. This is the beginning of the Communist regime.
June 24, 1918	Lenin establishes the Autonomous Volga German Workers Commune, which becomes the forerunner of the ASSR of the Volga Germans. It is founded in 1924.
1920-1923	This is a period of famine in Russia. Death

by starvation in the Volga- German colonies alone is estimated at 166,000, one third of the population. Assistance is provided by the American Relief Administration.

January 1924	Autonomous Socialist Soviet Republic of the Volga Germans is established.
1928–1933	*A second famine claims many lives throughout Russia.*
1928–1940	German farms and property are taken away by the Soviet government. Volga Germans are forced onto collective farms or they migrate to cities. This is the period of Stalinization.
September 1, 1939	*World War II begins.*
June 22, 1941	Nazi Germany invades Russia.
August 20, 1941	This is the beginning of exile and banishment of the Germans left in Russia. The Crimean Germans are deported.
August 28, 1941	A decree is put out ordering the deportation of the Volga Germans to the northeastern area of the Soviet Union. This includes Middle Asia and Siberia.
October 1941	The Germans in the North and South Caucasus are deported. Germans from St Petersbrug are also deported.
1991	*The Soviet Union falls.*

A Short History of Why Germans Went to Russia

GERMANY WAS NOT BROUGHT TOGETHER AS a nation until 1871. However, the German principalities and kingdoms shared a strong link with Russia. For centuries, Germans have lived inside of Russia's borders. They were especially drawn to the Baltic States where they were the landowners. During Peter the Great's reign, many Germans were given government positions. Under Elizabeth I, these positions were purged of foreign officers, primarily German officers.

On December 4, 1762, Catherine the Great, Tsarina of Russia, issued a manifesto asking Europeans to settle in Russia. There were few who answered the invitation. It was her second Manifesto of July 22, 1763 that offered freedom from military service, freedom from taxation, freedom of worship, and self-administration within the Russian Empire "for eternal time" that induced many Germans to migrate to Russia. Different enticements were used to get the emigrants to relocate to the Steppes of the Russian frontier. Stipends and loans were distributed to help with the relocation and establishment of colonies. Land was to be given as an inalienable and hereditary possession of the colony, though not to an individual for eternal time. Some colonists were allowed personal ownership. Catherine's timing couldn't have been better. The German peasants had suffered much through the Seven Years' War. Germany was a mix of 300 principalities and dukedoms, and these frequently changed hands politically and religiously.

With the opportunity to govern themselves and practice their own religion, thousands of Germans answered the call of Catherine's recruiters. With much effort, the recruiters mustered enough people, less than 500 families to populate 11 colonies on the Bergseite (hilly side) west of the Volga River and below the ancient settlement of Saratov. One of the recruiting teams consisted of a moderately successful trio of French men. They were Baron Jean de DeBoffe, Meusnier de Prescourt de Saint Laurent and Quentin Benjamin Coulhette d'Hauterive. The DeBoffe colonies were Bauer (Karamyshevka), Degott Kamey (oweag), Dietel (Oleshna), Franzosen (Rossoschi) Kautz (Wershinka), Kratzke (Potschennoje), Merkel (Makarovka), Rothammel (Pomjatnoje), Seewald (Werchnoje), Schuck (Grasnowatka), and Vollmer (Kopjonka). As you can see, these villages had Russian names, but they adopted names preferred by the colonists, which was usually the name of the leader of the colony.

Once recruited in Germany, the immigrants were gathered at various recruiting centers and organized for their travel to ports of departure along the northern coasts of Germany. Lubeck proved to be the best port. The vorstehers, or mayors, were then chosen from the more educated for their integrity, honesty, personal trust, and respect acquired from their fellow travelers. They were given responsibility for an assigned group of people. From these ports, the colonists sailed to a processing center at the mouth of the Neva Riva, in the harbor of St. Petersburg. Oranienbaum is an alternate name given for the center and is named for the local palace of Peter the Great. Here, the colonists were required to take the "Solemn Oath" to the Russian crown. Processing for the colonists could take weeks or months. Supplies were then purchased in Oranienbaum, and the colonists would then begin the final leg of the journey to their final destination with assigned escorting officers. The colonists had to winter along the way and were often put up in the houses of the Russian peasants. Many of the sickly and elderly died along this hazardous journey to their colony's location along the Volga.

Arrival at the colony sites was disastrous, to say the least. They had been promised finished houses in their new villages, but when they arrived, there was nothing. Instead, the Russian officers halted the wagons at predetermined sites on the barren sites and pointed out the location for the yet to be built colony. Because the colonists had arrived late in the summer there was little time to prepare for winter. Most of the colonists spent the winter in dugouts, or semlyanka, patterned after winter homes of nearby tribesmen. The Dietel colonists of my grandmother arrived on July 1, 1767.

What a difficult beginning. Many died of cold, illness, or starvation. The first three years were years of hardship, but those who survived persevered and eventually prospered. By the time the Volga Germans began migrating again, this time to the United States, there were about 1,700,000 hard-working, prosperous colonists.

The Women in my Life

VOLGA GERMAN WOMEN ARE TOUGH. I know this first hand because I grew up surrounded by them. There was my grandmother Susanna Kinsfather Nab. She had five stepmothers when growing up in Russia. She never said what happened to them all, but I'm going to guess childbirth with no doctors, cold and pneumonia, or being worked to death. Women in Russia worked in the fields like slaves, had their babies at the end of a field, wrapped them up, and went back to work. The fields were sometimes very far away from the villages and at harvest time, the men could be gone for a month. The women would stay behind to look after the children, the livestock, and the house. My Grandma Nab never would talk much about Russia. She did, however, tell me that one harvest the men were gone a very long time in far away fields, and she was running out of meat. She politely went out to the pigs, sat on one, slit its throat, and butchered it herself! She told me this in German because she never spoke English. She did understand English, so she spoke to us in German, and we answered in English! It sounds rather strange, but it worked perfectly well and seemed normal to me.

Grandma had very lovely white hair that went halfway down her back. She wore it in a twisted bun on the top of her head. I only saw it down once when my Aunt Esther was helping her brush it. I was probably about 10 at the time. I wondered out loud to my Aunt about why Grandma didn't try a different hairstyle. Aunt Esther said that Grandma Nab would never be able to wear it any other way because she had been struck by lightning on the top of her head while working in the fields. She had survived, but the hair on top of her head was gone! She survived being struck by lightning. Now, that is tough.

I didn't get to know my grandmother until she was in her 70s and living in a little three-room house in town. My dad was the youngest of seven children and I was his youngest, so everyone seemed quite old to me. I didn't get to ask any questions about what it was like in Russia and why they left. My father told me that the Bolsheviks had started to overrun the German villages, burning, raping, hanging women, cutting off their breasts, and pulling out their gold teeth. So, Grandma Nab had seen too much and lived through tragedy after tragedy. She was harsh and could be pretty mean. She was rather nice to me, but I was just a child. When she started yelling at Grandpa in German and shaking her fist, we all found somewhere else to be. She wasn't cooking the big meals or baking so much when I knew her. She left that to her daughters and daughter-in-laws. She was probably a great cook though because her two daughters were fantastic.

My mother's mother, Grandma Bauer was basically lost to me also. She moved to Portland, Oregon in 1941. I saw her every few years when she came for a visit. When I knew her she was a happy, accepting free spirit. She had nine children of whom seven survived. She was only a year old when she came to America so, although she could speak German, she was much more Americanized. We all loved her very much. She had the greatest laugh and loved to visit all her children and grandchildren. She had to be pretty tough too, because my Grandpa Bauer was an alcoholic and he beat the girls and probably Grandma. He lost the beautiful farm they had because of his gambling and drinking. They moved to town and he was a cook for a while. They lived in my hometown of Torrington on a farm for a while until Aunt Mary, Aunt Katherine, and Aunt Doris convinced him to go to Vancouver because there were good jobs in the Jantzen woolen mills. He got on the bus on December 31, 1940 to go to Portland without telling Grandma. My mother saw him getting on the bus. She was with my dad and Grandpa Nab. It was her wedding day. Her parents had not gone to the justice of the peace with her, but had given written permission because my mom was only 18 years old.

My mom and dad rushed out to Grandma's little farm to tell her that papa had taken off. They didn't hear from him for two months, and then he told Grandma to sell everything and come out to Vancouver. She did it too, all by herself. We never did figure out why he didn't tell grandma where he was going. What difference could it have made? He left her and she would have known nothing if mom hadn't seen him get on that bus. They did end up doing well in Oregon and lived on a small Orchard farm that grandpa bought and fixed up. He passed away in 1956. Grandma never remarried, but she had a boyfriend or two. She scandalized all five of her daughters in 1961 when she came roaring in to visit us on a motorcycle with her new biker friend. Mom and Aunt Esther Schmidt told her to get rid of the guy or they would disown her. She eventually saw the light and dropped him. But I always thought she was pretty brave and cool to give it a whirl. Grandma Bauer was famous in our family for a great line she used on her son Uncle Hank. She was visiting him and staying at his house. He had three very unruly children and he apologized to her and said he should probably put her in a cage to protect her from them. She stared at him for a moment and then in German said "Hank, if you can teach bears to dance, surely you can teach children to behave!" And one last thing: Grandma worked in the shipyards during World War 11 when so many of the men were away serving in the War. She was one of the "Rosie the Riveter women" I didn't get to sample her cooking very often, but all her girls were fantastic cooks and they learned from her.

I knew my aunts and their cooking and I want to share this with you.

Dad had two sisters and Mom had five. Back then, girls were named Mary, Esther, and Katherine. Dad had Mary and Esther. Mom had Mary, Esther, Katherine, Doris, and Pauline. Pauline died when she was 12 from polio and my mother was then the youngest. Her name is Helen. These women taught me a love of good food and the love it can bring back to you from the people you have grace your table. In the rest of the book, I will combine family stories, good times, and recipes for original Volga German food and also favorite American food that naturally crept onto our table.

The Flood

I LIVED ON A FARM IN WYOMING. I guess I should say that I lived on several farms. You see, we never owned a farm—we rented farms in southeastern Wyoming outside of a little town named Torrington. I grew up with disaster on my mind. What was going to strike the farm? Would it be hail, tornado, flood, wind, weeds, pests, or drought? While I was growing up on these farms, all these disastrous things happened to us at one time or another. When I was five, we lived on a nice farm on Cherry Creek three miles outside of Torrington. We are Volga Germans and my father, Harold Nab, was the second generation of the German immigration from Russia. He was trying to become a successful farmer and raise us to be true and loyal Americans, just as we were once loyal Russian citizens. My dad was truly a handsome man with china blue eyes, black hair, and the most beguiling smile. My mother Helen was petite and only five feet two -inches tall. She had deep rich brown hair and lovely hazel eyes, and she had the energy and stamina in her small frame for two men. Harold and Helen were a truly handsome, fun-loving, hard-working couple. Then, there were my two brothers, Tim and Ron. Ron, the oldest, was nine years older than me and mischievous and fun loving. He was very outgoing, made friends easily, and had curly red hair and the same china blue eyes as Dad. The red hair came from Papa Bauer, my mom's dad. Tim was quiet and serious. He was the middle child and three years older than I was. He liked farming and being with Dad. He had dark brown hair and hazel eyes. And then there is me, Rebecca. I am the youngest and the only girl. I had dirty blonde hair that got darker as I got older, and I have grass green eyes, except that the left one has a blob of brown in the upper corner. I was more quiet and shyer than my brother Tim was. I was sick a lot until I finally had my tonsils removed and was so thin that elastic was put in all my clothes. I was born in 1950. I'm describing my family for you so that you understand that none of us looks like the other, but nonetheless, we were very close. I should add that my father did have a fiery temper that could explode out of nowhere. For the most part though, he joked with us a lot and hummed church hymns all day long. He would hum a little and then sing a little. He liked singing "The Old Rugged Cross" and "What A Friend We Have In Jesus."

My first memory as a child is not a good one. In 1955, there was a terrible storm and Cherry Creek and the North Platte River started to flood. Our house was close to the creek and the creek spilled over its banks, covered the fields and pastures, and began to fill our basement. This was in late June. My brother Ron remembers the flood much better than I do because he was 14. He told me that he and Dad had spent the afternoon cleaning up the yard because the landowners had installed a bathroom for us and we needed to haul away the leftover garbage. The crops looked so beautiful. The corn was knee high and ready to ditch; the hay was ready to cut; the sugar beets were ready to ditch; and the beans looked good too. When the storm came in, Ron says that the roar sounded like a squadron of jets in the sky. It hailed and rained for two hours and 10 minutes, and then there was nothing left of those beautiful crops. The storm covered the whole valley. The water came tumbling and roaring down Cherry Creek filled with dead livestock and hay bales and stopped up the outlet to the bridge. That's why the water went through our yard and the basement of the house. The water went in one basement window and out another on the other side of the house.

My dad drove down the road about two miles to pick up his mother and father to drive them to the Dickens farmhouse, which was up on a high hill. He came back to get the rest of us. It was raining hard with lightening, thunder, and the always-present Wyoming wind. We just barely got across the Cherry Creek Bridge to make it to the Dickens place. Water was gushing over the wood plank bridge. There was water everywhere and there was a heavy darkness. Dad wanted to go back to check on his new herd of cattle, but he couldn't make it. He had bought them the day before and put them in the far southeast pasture. He was afraid they were all drowned, but we could hear them plaintively bawling all through the night. It was heart wrenching to hear them and not be able to find them or help them.

I know we spent the night with the neighbors, and in the daylight, we went back to the devastation. The bridge over Cherry Creek on the highway was damaged, and all traffic was stopped. No one could get into or out of Torrington. We had to borrow Mr. Dickens' tractor to get back down the hill to the house. Dad took us home and then took off across the fields to see if he could help the cattle. He found them crowded forlornly, heads down, on a little knoll, but they were alive. He hurried to town, rented a big pump and pumped the water off the pasture and back into the creek so the cattle could get off that knoll. Then, he came back to our poor little house. The basement was full of water, the stairs were under water, and the water was creeping into the kitchen. Mom's beautiful cedar chest was floating around and my dolls had drowned in the dirty water. Dad got the pump and a big hose and pumped the water out through a window.

My Uncle Ted and Aunt Alvina, Uncle Riney and Aunt Esther, and Uncle Charlie and Aunt Esther came from their own farms to help us dig out. They scooped mud out with shovels and dragged all the reeking, rotting food and clothing outside. Mom was crying and asking, "What are we going to do?" and Dad was saying that it would get better and we would be all right. Her confirmation dress, which had been so white and beautiful, had been stored in the cedar chest. In the end the dress couldn't be saved. All our birth certificates were soaked and mud stained. Mom was able to dry these and I still have mine. Whenever I need to use it, I see those tiny mud stained footprints and live that night over again. Mom, who had lost so much of her life that day, was more worried about my favorite doll Suzy. Suzy had a rubber body and some sort of shredded rubber stuffing. Mom sat in the yard trying to dry out that doll's guts, but she was not successful. I probably was crying and she wanted to make me feel better. Suzy couldn't be saved. Nothing in the basement was saved. However, that wasn't the worst of it.

Dad lost all the crops. He had borrowed a lot of money from the bank to run the Cherry Creek farm, and I remember vividly how frightened I felt inside. What would become of us? Where would we get money to pay back the bank or buy groceries, or clothes, or anything? I heard Mom and Dad talk long into the nights about what to do, and finally, Dad announced that he was loading up the beet harvesting equipment and traveling 100 miles to the Morton ranch outside of Douglas Wyoming to harvest their beet crop. I have no idea how he got this job, but I know he was gone for six weeks.

Every Sunday during those six weeks, my mother made lovely fried chicken, potato salad, light rye bread, desserts, sandwiches—all kinds of wonderful food—German or American. She loaded up the car with three children, food, and clean clothes for dad. I know she had never driven that far by herself before. She had to have been terrified, but she never let on. About halfway to Douglas there was a large cottonwood tree with a picnic table sitting underneath. Mom always stopped there and gave us a lunch out of the big box she had packed. I only remember the fried chicken and how good it tasted while sitting under that tree in the crisp autumn. We didn't linger long under that cottonwood because we knew Dad was waiting eagerly to see us. I don't remember fighting with my brothers on those trips because I think we knew mom was stretched to the limit. Dad was so glad to see all of us on those Sundays. He was staying in a bunkhouse that was old and sparsely furnished, and had holes in the roof. Dad made big jokes about being able to watch the stars and moon at night. He lived for those Sundays. He was hungry, lonely, and tired. My mom and her good German food soothed his soul. He would eat and eat and tell Mom repeatedly how good it all was. Mom made kuchen, German chocolate cake, doughnuts, bread, homemade dills, and kraut birok, (a German cabbage bun), and everything was good. She made everything from scratch because in 1955 there were not box mixes and frozen entrees. If you cooked, you made everything yourself. Dad would wash up outside at a pump and change clothes and sit and talk with us and eat. We never stayed too long because it was a long trip back home in the dark, and my brothers had to go school the next day. I bet that my Dad felt so lonely after we left and probably worried about our long trip home. There was no Interstate 25 like there is today. We were on two-lane winding narrow road for 100 miles. At the end of six weeks my father came home a little thinner but grateful to have his family back. And the triumph? Dad was able to go to the bank, lay a check down on the loan officer's desk, and pay back the money he had borrowed. He was able to borrow again the next year so we could keep farming.

This is my first memory of growing up.

Kraut Birok is a Volga German specialty. My people brought this dish with them from Russia to America. It is sweet dough filled with onion, hamburger, and cabbage. It travels well because it is self-contained. You don't need anything else for your lunch if you have these. In Russia, the fields were far from the village, so they probably developed this sandwich for a midday meal to be eaten right there in the fields. You can eat them hot or cold, but hot is better. These take most of the day to make because of raising the dough and chopping the cabbage. If you are traveling in Nebraska or southeastern Wyoming, you will be able to buy them in sandwich shops where they call them Runzas.

CABBAGE BUNS OR KRAUT BEROK

Serving Size: 4 ounce

Total Servings: 12

1 large head of cabbage finely shredded

1 medium chopped onion

1/4 cup water

11/2 pounds of hamburger

1 teaspoon salt

1 teaspoon pepper

Sweet dough

1. Mix the cabbage and onion, and then add salt and pepper to taste. Add the water.

2. Steam the mixture in a large kettle until tender. Drain off the water.

3. Fry 11/2 pounds of hamburger. Cook until done. Thoroughly drain off the grease.

4. Add the hamburger to the cooked cabbage; mix it all together.

5. Make your favorite sweet dough recipe or the one that follows this recipe and then roll out the dough to about 1/8 inch in thickness. Cut into 3 x 3 inch squares. Fill the squares with a couple of tablespoons of the cabbage mixture. Bring up the sides of the dough and pinch them together. Be sure to seal the squares on each side.

6. Put the pinched sides down in a well-greased pan. Let them rise for 20 minutes. Bake at 350 degrees for 25 to 30 minutes or until golden brown. Serve hot. You can

use more cabbage or more meat depending on what you like.

Mother's Tip

After you cook the hamburger and drain the grease, rinse the meat with hot water and thoroughly drain it again to get rid of all the grease. This keeps the bun from becoming soggy or grease soaked.

If you are limited for time, there are sweet dough box mixes you can buy in a grocery store that work well for this recipe.

After you take the cabbage buns out of the oven and while they are still warm, you can brush them with melted butter to give them a golden brown appearance.

SWEET DOUGH RECIPE FOR CABBAGE BUNS

Serving Size: 4 ounce

Total Servings: 12

1 cup milk, scalded (To scald milk, heat it to just below the boiling point when tiny bubbles appear at the edge of the saucepan.)

1 cup boiling water

1/2 cup sugar

1 teaspoon salt

2 packages yeast

1/2 cup melted oleo or butter

5 cups flour

2 beaten eggs

1. Put boiled water, sugar, and salt in a large bowl and mix.
2. Add the yeast, melted butter, and 2 cups of the flour.
3. Beat with an electric mixer for 2 minutes.
4. Add eggs. Mix by hand until smooth.

Add the remaining cups of flour. Knead the dough for at least 5 minutes. Let the dough rise for half an hour. Roll out the dough until it is 1/8 inch thick and make the cabbage buns. The buns will be about 3 inches square with a golden brown color.

Noodle Head

THIS STORY IS LEGENDARY. **I** BELIEVE everyone in my family has told this tale to someone to impress upon them the fearsomeness of my grandmother.

As I said earlier, grandma Nab was rather stern.

Emil, Bill, Walter, Ted, Mary, Esther, and my dad Harold were working in the fields on their farm. They were still young children. Uncle Walter was the oldest and probably had to work the hardest. The tribe trooped in from the fields, washed up, and sat down around the old wood table. Grandma came to the table with a huge pot of homemade chicken and noodles. She put it down in the middle of the table and asked Grandpa to say the blessing for the food. Uncle Walter was ravenous and he just couldn't wait for the "Amen." Before Grandpa could finish, Uncle Walter reached out and started to take a ladle full of noodles, broth, and butterballs. Grandma Nab moved faster than anyone thought possible. She grabbed the ladle and conked Uncle Walter over the head with it. Dad said that Walter had noodles and juice streaming down his hair and face. When Dad would tell this story, he laughed so hard that tears came to his eyes and rolled down his cheeks. I know he saw that picture of Uncle Walter in his head every time he told the story. The moral? Always wait to hear the Amen! The recipe for those famous noodles follows.

CHICKEN SOUP WITH YELLOW EGG NOODLES

1. A whole cleaned chicken should be simmering in a large, covered kettle while you roll out the noodles.

2. Cover the chicken completely with water. Add 2 teaspoons salt and 1 bay leaf in the water for flavor.

3. Bring the water and the chicken to a boil, then lower the heat and simmer.

4. Remove the chicken from the pot after simmering on low heat for $1\frac{1}{2}$ hours and skim the grease from the top of the broth.

5. Use the broth to cook the noodles.

YELLOW EGG NOODLES

Serving Size: 4 ounce

Total Servings: 6

3 eggs

1 teaspoon salt

2 cups flour

2 tablespoon milk

1. Mix the ingredients together. You may need to add more milk or more flour to get the right consistency. The dough should be a little stiff.

2. Roll the dough flat on a floured cutting board. Then roll it up like a newspaper and then slice it very thin, about 1/8 inch in width with a sharp knife.

3. Separate the noodles and fluff them up. Pick the noodles up in cupped hands and gently let them separate and fall back onto the floured cutting board. Do this 4 or 5 times. The noodles will naturally pick up some flour from the cutting board and will not stick together.

4. Dry them on your chopping board until you are ready to drop the noodles into the pot of chicken and broth. The flour that is left on the noodles from rolling them out will thicken the broth.

5. Cook the broth and noodles for about 15 minutes on medium heat.

Let Them Eat Cake

UNCLE WALTER AND AUNT EDITH CAME from Saginaw, MI in the summer of 1957 for a visit with their brothers and sisters. My dad was Uncle Walter's younger brother. They stayed a few days at all of our houses. The children—Edwin, Roy, and Janice—enjoyed coming to our farm because Ron, Tim, and I were the same ages.

It was a Saturday and Mom needed to go to town to buy groceries. Saturday was always grocery day. She decided to make a German chocolate cake before we went off to Torrington. It would be dessert for everyone for supper. She had a gallon of vanilla ice cream to go with it. Mom mixed up the cake and put it in a big 9 x13-inch pan so it would stretch to feed 10 people. She iced it with the gooey pecan caramel topping and then put it on the counter. Off we went to town. We got back late in the afternoon and hurried in with our bags of groceries. And what did we find? A table surrounded by men and boys, an empty cake pan, and only a little dab of ice cream left in the bucket. Dad said he thought Mom made it for an afternoon snack, and after all, they had worked hard playing baseball in the pasture by the house. There was no dessert with dinner, but the men were pretty full anyway. My regret is that Mom and I got no cake.

GERMAN CHOCOLATE CAKE

Serving Size: 6 ounce

Total Servings: 10

1 package German sweet chocolate

1/2 cup boiling water

1 teaspoon vanilla

1 cup buttermilk

4 egg yolks unbeaten

2 1/2 cups sifted cake flour

2 cups sugar

1 teaspoon baking soda

1 cup butter

1/2 teaspoon salt

4 egg whites stiffly beaten

1. Bring the 1/2 cup of water to a boil. Pull it off stove and drop the German sweet chocolate into it and let it melt and then let it cool.

2. Cream the butter and sugar until fluffy.

3. Add egg yolks one at a time and beat well after you add each yolk.

4. Add the melted chocolate and the vanilla, mixing well.

5. Sift together the salt, baking soda, and flour. Add the flour mixture alternately with the buttermilk to the chocolate mixture, beating well after each addition and until smooth.

6. Fold in the beaten egg whites.

7. Pour the mixture into three 8- or 9-inch round layer pans. The bottom of the pans should be lined with wax paper or sprayed liberally with Pam cooking oil. Bake at 350 degrees for 30 to 40 minutes.

8. Cool and frost.

GOOEY CARAMEL PECAN FROSTING

Serving Size: Yields 2/3 cups

Total Servings: Covers 9 -inch cake

1 cup evaporated milk

3 egg yolks

1 teaspoon vanilla

1 cup sugar

1/4 pound margarine

11/3 cup Bakers Angel Flake coconut or another brand of coconut

1 cup chopped pecans

1. Combine all of the ingredients, except the coconut and pecans. Cook and stir over medium heat until the mixture thickens. This takes about 12 minutes.

2. Add the coconut and the pecans. Beat until thick enough to spread.

Mother's Tip

This cake and frosting is what we requested the most for our special birthday cake. Aunts, uncles, and cousins were invited for each person's birthday every year. The birthday celebrant got to choose what kind of cake he or she wanted and a flavor of ice cream. The party was usually in the evening when farm work was done. This tradition is still going strong to this day. Each person's birthday is very special in our family.

Arm and Window

ALTHOUGH I WAS ONLY TWO YEARS old at the time, I swear I remember most of the story I'm about to tell you.

Mom and I were in the basement. It was bath time, and because we didn't have an indoor bathroom, we used a big old oval tin tub that Mom drug out and filled with buckets of heated water. Mom was on her knees scrubbing the heck out of my skin with homemade lye soap when Dad appeared at the top of the stairs. He had the car keys to give to her, but I can't remember why she needed them. Dad tossed the keys down to the stairs to her, and she caught them and tossed them back up to him. They were young and just horsing around. I don't know how many times they tossed the keys back and forth, but they went wide on one toss and Mom had to lunge to catch them. There were several long windows in the basement and Mom's arm went right through the window, but she was okay. However, when she jerked her arm back through the glass a jagged piece of broken glass ripped across her bicep and opened up a big gash. I remember that Dad was pretty hysterical but Mom stayed calm. She took the towel she was going to dry me with and wrapped it tightly around her arm and said "Harold, take me to the hospital right now. I'm losing a lot of blood." Dad retrieved the keys and they sped off to the hospital and left me sitting in the tub. I didn't cry. I just sat there until my brother Ron, who would have been 11 at the time, found me and lifted me out of the tin tub, dried me off, and put some clothes on me. Then, Ron, Tim, and I just sat in a row on the couch waiting for our parents to come back to us.

Mom came home with 12 stitches, a sore arm, and teasing from my brothers about what trouble horse play can get you into. We were all kind of frightened though because Mom had bled everywhere, and she was so white when she came home. Throwing anything down the stairs to be caught was forever banned in our house from then on.

It's hard to come up with any kind of recipe for this story because it's not about food, it's about how quickly bad or good things can happen.

I thought that for the fun of it, I would give you Spring Fling Cake.

SPRING FLING CAKE

Serving Size: 6 ounce

Total Servings: 10

1 box lemon cake mix with pudding in it

1 16-ounce can mandarin oranges plus juice

1. Follow the instructions for the cake mix, and then add the mandarin oranges and the juice.

2. Pour the cake mix into two 9-inch round cake pans that have been sprayed with Pam or another cooking spray and bake for 35 minutes at 350 degrees in a preheated oven.

Frosting

1 3-ounce package lemon instant pudding

1 15-ounce can crushed pineapple with juice

9 ounce carton of Cool Whip

1. Make the pudding following the instructions on the box.

2. Mix together the pudding and crushed pineapple.

3. Add Cool Whip.

4. Frost the first 9-inch layer of the cake. Place the second 9-inch cake layer on top of this layer and spread the rest of the frosting over the whole cake.

5. Refrigerate for 1 hour before serving.

Alvin, Simon, and Theodore

$\mathcal{S}$TRANGE TITLE FOR A CHRISTMAS STORY to be sure, but you will understand as I tell you about Christmas with the Nabs.

First of all, Helen, my mother does not remember any of her childhood. She can't really remember anything until around the age of 15. Growing up with an alcoholic father was traumatic enough to cause her to block it all out. So, I cannot draw upon her memories of past holidays. I will instead, tell you about Christmas in the 1950s on a farm in Wyoming.

Mom and Dad both tried to give my brothers and me the best possible Christmas. I'm sure that seeing our joy and wonder helped them to have a little childlike wonder themselves, which is something they never got to experience with the harsh realities that they lived with while growing up. When Ron, Tim, and I got on the bus and went off to school in November and December, Mom would lug out her sewing machine and patterns and whip up skirts, blouses, and weskits for me. While we were gone, she would make all kinds of candies and cookies. She made caramels, fudge, caramel corn, divinity, date pinwheels, and fruitcakes. The caramels would be cut in -inch squares and wrapped in waxed paper with the ends twisted shut. Mother had to do all this sewing and baking while we were gone and hide all her endeavors in the closet in her bedroom. If she had left any of the candies out too soon before Christmas, we would have inhaled it, and she would have had to start over. During the holidays in our little community, people would just stop by to visit and wish you a "Happy Christmas." This would start about two weeks before the actual holiday. When friends, neighbors, and relatives stopped by, they always had a little something to give you such as a box of chocolate covered cherries, a bottle of Mogen David Wine, or homemade cookies and candies. Mom had to have something to reciprocate with, so she had to keep us away from it until the visiting began.

On Ron's birthday, December 17, Mom and I and sometimes Dad would go to the Christmas tree lot in Torrington and get a tree. My Father, being a rather flamboyant character, would ask me to pick the best tree I could find. I would go round and round, but always came back to the thick, well-shaped scotch pines. They were the most expensive, and Mom would say "No Harold, absolutely not. It's too expensive to just dry up and be thrown out." But Dad would say, "So Slim, would you like this tree?" Well, I would just nod, as I was a very quiet child, but my heart would soar. A beautiful tree for our living room with Grandma Bauer's delicate German glass ornaments on it was just what I would like. Dad would put the tree into the back of the pickup, and we would lovingly take it home. Dad would help us get it in the stand so it stood straight and proud, and then the rest was up to Mom and me. I actually did make red and green paper chains and popcorn chains to help fill in the tree. The last thing was tinsel. I would start out carefully separating the strands of tinsel and put three or four strands on a branch. By this time, however, I was getting impatient to be done so that we could put the presents out, so I would just throw the last of the tinsel and see where it landed. The tree was decorated at last, and Mother would carefully put out the presents, arranging them all around the tree. Dad would take over; he would put the star on the top of the tree and plug in the lights. There were colored lights in the star, and it was a lovely sight! Dad would then make Mother annoyed to no end because he would get down on the floor and start picking up boxes and looking at the names and encourage us to shake the presents and make guesses as to what we were getting. Mother said he was more of a child than all the rest of us put together! When she finally had enough of his playfulness, she had us sit down to a supper of sandwiches and soup. She was tired and would make a simple meal on tree day. Besides, We usually had a coterie of relatives stop by around seven in the evening to wish Ron a happy birthday and share cake and ice cream with us.

Christmas Eve would arrive at last, and we had our traditions. Some families have the argument about when to open the presents— Christmas Eve or Christmas Day. There was no argument at our house. We attended candlelight services at our Presbyterian church. I liked this service so much! There was a huge tree up front of the church to the right of the alter by the choir. There were candles and greenery on every ledge of the stained glass windows down both sides of the church, and there were red poinsettias everywhere. We would sing song after song such as "O Little Town of Bethlehem," "Joy to the World," or "O Come All Ye Faithful." The minister would read Luke 2, which tells the birth of Jesus. There would be a closing prayer, and we were off to Grandma and Grandpa Nab's house. We always stopped to see them on Christmas Eve and visit and give them each a present. Ron, Tim, and I would fidget a lot, but we didn't dare say anything. Children did not tell parents what to do back then. We just kept quiet until Dad said it was time to go on home and have a "little Christmas" before Christmas Eve was over. When we got home, the tree was lit up and Ron, being the oldest, got to hand out the presents. Dad always had a pile of presents around him because he would be watching all of us and not to get around to his own. He usually received a lot of cologne or ties or long underwear anyway. When I was nine years old, I had the best Christmas ever. I don't know what came over Mom and Dad, but they gave me a record player and three records. It was a little red and white 45 player on a black metal stand that had slots for records on the bottom. Can you imagine my delight? The three records were "Thumbelina," "Adeste Fidelis," and "The Chipmunk Song." I got other things too, like a couple of skirts and vests that Mom had sewed for me, but those records and player became an obsession. I played them over and over again until I had to go to bed. I played them all day on Christmas. I learned all the words by heart and so did everyone else in the family. I particularly liked "The Chipmunk Song" with, you guessed it, Simon, Theodore, and Alvin. My brothers groaned out loud every time I put it on. Mom went to the kitchen to get away from it, and Dad just laughed and laughed and sang along with me. Mom finally made me move the record player into the bedroom and shut the door. I bet they all still could hear the guy yelling "Alvin!" and the chipmunks' cute little voices harmonizing about the plane loop de loops. I don't know what happened to my record player and three precious records, but I wish I had them still. I bet I could make Mom have a spasm of laughing if I played that little ditty today! My brothers still talk about how crazy I was about that record.

When I had my own home and started making my own cookies and candies for Christmas, I started a tradition that still is going strong. I took a cake recipe of Mother's that she got from Grandma Bauer and instead of putting it in a cake pan, I put it in tiny little loaf pans and gave it away as a gift. Mom called this recipe fruitcake, but that has a very bad connotation, and it isn't fruitcake at all. It's more of a spice cake. I now call it Holiday Cake, and after all these years of hoarding the recipe, I will tell all. I have only seen this recipe once before, but it had eggs and mine doesn't. It was called prairie fruitcake and was from the plains of Nebraska. I'll also give you my Mother's Krazy Korn recipe, homemade caramels, and the marshmallow popcorn balls that my son Ryan just adores.

MARSHMALLOW POPCORN BALLS

Serving Size: 8 ounce

Total Servings: 12 to 16

1 6-ounce package popcorn

1 16-ounce package marshmallows

1 stick margarine

2 teaspoons anise flavoring

1. Melt the marshmallows and margarine in the top of a double boiler. When melted, remove from heat and add the anise flavoring.

2. Pour the marshmallow mixture over the popcorn that has been popped and the unpopped seeds removed. You will need a large mixing bowl for this.

3. Form the popcorn mixture into balls about the size of a softball.

4. This makes about 12 to 16 popcorn balls, depending on how big you make them. When you are finished making the popcorn balls, put each one in a ziplock plastic sandwich bag and seal so they will stay fresh.

Mother's Tip

If you do not care for licorice, orange flavoring is good too. You can also make this recipe with no flavorings and it will have just a nice creamy marshmallow flavor.

MOM'S HOLIDAY CAKE

Serving Size: 3 ounce

Total Servings: 12

1 1/2 cups applesauce

1/2 cup shortening melted

1 cup sugar

1/2 teaspoon each of cinnamon, nutmeg, cloves, and allspice
pinch of salt

1 teaspoon soda

3 1/2 cups flour

1 cup dates

1 cup raisins

1 cup walnuts

Enough milk for a thick batter

1. Combine and cream the first three ingredients.
2. In a separate bowl, sift together all the dry ingredients.
3. Add the flour, a little at a time, to the creamed ingredient. Alternate this with a little milk so it doesn't become too thick.
4. Then add raisins, dates, and nuts.
5. Bake in a 375 degree oven for 45 minutes.

Mother's Tip

1. You can substitute the shortening in this recipe with canola oil for a healthier recipe.

2. This is a recipe that I've never given out. I think it was my grandmother's and she gave it to my Mother. I triple this recipe and put the batter in small little loaf pans. I make it at Christmas time, give it away for gifts, and use it at parties and dinners during the holidays. Sometimes I send a few loaves to Mom because she loves this cake so much.

CHRISTMAS CARAMELS

Serving Size: 1 ounce

Total Servings: 30

2 cups sugar

1 1/3 cups corn syrup

2 cups cream

3/4 cup evaporated milk

2 tablespoons butter

2 tablespoons vanilla

Pinch of salt

1. In a heavy saucepan, put the sugar, corn syrup, a pinch of salt, and half the cream.

2. Bring to the boiling point, stirring occasionally.

3. Very gradually add the remaining cream and evaporated milk. Do this so gradually that the mixture never ceases boiling.

4. Cook about 15 minutes and add the butter; continue cooking to soft ball stage (234 degrees) for a soft caramel. For a firm caramel, cook a few minutes longer (250 degrees). Stir gently but constantly throughout cooking. A candy thermometer should be used.

5. Add vanilla.

6. Total cooking time is about 35 minutes.

7. Pour into shallow 9 x 13-inch pan.

8. After you have poured the caramels into the pan, let cool and set for about 15 minutes. Cut into squares and wrap in waxed paper.

9. You can double this recipe, but use two 9 x 13-inch pans.

KARO KRAZY KRUNCH

My mother has been making this treat since I was a child. She only makes it at Christmas. She knows how much I enjoy this recipe so she makes bags and bags of it and sends it to me to share with my own family.

Serving Size: 8 ounce

Total Servings: 10

11/3 cups pecans

2/3 cups almonds

1 6-ounce bag of popcorn, popped and any unpopped kernels removed. You can use an air popper, or you can even use microwave popcorn if it is plain.

11/3 cups granulated sugar

1/2 cup margarine or butter

1/2 cup light Karo syrup

1 teaspoon vanilla

1. Mix the popcorn and nuts and set aside while you are mixing and cooking the syrup.

2. Combine the sugar, butter, and syrup in a 11/2 quart saucepan. Bring it to a boil over medium heat, stirring constantly. Continue 10 to 15 minutes, stirring occasionally or until the mixture turns into a light caramel color.

3. Remove from the heat and stir in the vanilla.

4. Pour over the popcorn and peanuts. Mix to coat evenly.

5. Spread the krazy krunch out to dry and then break it apart and store it in a tightly covered container. This is quite addictive, so make a lot!

The Dogs and I

FROM THE TIME I CAN REMEMBER anything, I remember having dogs. Dad would let us have a dog, but we couldn't have a pony or a horse because he said, "They're hay burners and don't pay for their keep." Now, dogs were different. They could survive on scraps, and keep the fox out of the hen house at night and scare off varmints or humans in general.

People say you are either a dog person or a cat person, but I really didn't have to choose. The cats lived in the barn, killed mice, and had a nice life with a pan of cow's milk every night. The dogs roamed wherever they wanted and ate table scraps and slept under cars or in the barn. Dogs and cats were not allowed in the house.

When I was about 10 years old, I got a puppy that I named Tramp. He was a mixed breed, but was a beautiful caramel color with a white chest and a big white tip on his tail. Tramp went everywhere with me. I had my bicycle by this time, and he ran along side of me. He helped me mow the lawn, rake leaves, and feed cows. He was my sidekick. We had a two-lane highway that ran by our farmhouse, and Tramp liked to cross the highway and explore the neighbor's fields. One morning, he was crossing the highway and got hit by a motorcycle. He was spun around and hit very hard. My brothers and I saw it happen and were just paralyzed with fear as we watched Tramp drag himself off the highway and back into the yard. I was bawling my eyes out and yelling for Mom. She came running out, took one look at Tramp and thought that he wasn't going to be with us for long. His front shoulder and leg were just useless. The leg was dragging the ground and she didn't know if he also had internal injuries. She had the boys carry Tramp into the barn, make him a nice bed of straw, and give him a little water. She thought he would be gone in a few hours. He did not die in a few hours or in a few days. Tramp actually lay in the barn for weeks. Mom cooked for him. She gave him cow's liver, tongue, and heart. She said he needed blood-rich meats to get strong. We hand fed him, cleaned up after him, and hoped for a miracle, but I knew in my heart that his leg was paralyzed because it wouldn't move at all. I was so sad for my Tramp, but one day he came out of the barn all by himself! It must have been about a month and his leg was dragging and useless. Mother fashioned a sling for him and pulled his leg up to his shoulder as if it was a chicken wing. We had to keep making him new slings because he would lose them or wear them out. His leg would be raw from losing the sling and dragging, but he was alive and managing on three legs. This story has a happy ending. Eventually, Tramp's leg pulled up and stayed there. He became a very able three-legged dog as he got around like any dog. His funny little quirk was going under the electric fence that Dad would put around a field so he could turn the cattle in for forage. Tramp would hop under it just fine, but his tail was too high and would always hit the fence and Tramp would yelp, and Dad would know that the fence was working. Mom was my heroine in this story. Why, when she was so busy with the farm and children, did she show such love and kindness to Tramp? I believe it was because she loved us children so much that she couldn't stand to see us brokenhearted. My mother is actually the most loving, kind person I have ever known, and I wish we could all be a little more like her.

And to all the dogs I have loved and been loved by—thank you Cocoa, Tramp, Twan, Misty, Lucky, Shep, Emily, Queenie, and Dakota.

I think liver is a good choice for a recipe here because Mom helped Tramp get well with liver, heart, and tongue.

TEMPTING LIVER AND ONIONS

Serving Size: 8 ounce

Total Servings: 4

2 pound sliced beef liver

1 1/2 cups milk, or as needed

1/4 cup butter, divided

2 large Vidalia onions, sliced into rings

2 cups flour

Salt and pepper

1. Gently rinse the liver slices under cold water and place in a medium bowl. Pour in enough milk to cover the liver and soak for at least an hour. This step is important because it takes the bitterness out of the liver.

2. Melt 2 tablespoons of butter in a large skillet over medium heat. Separate the onion rings and sauté them in butter until they are soft.

3. Remove the onions and melt the remaining butter in the skillet.

4. Season the flour with salt and pepper, and put it into a shallow dish. Drain the milk from the liver. Dredge the liver in the flour to coat it liberally.

5. When the butter has melted, turn the heat to medium high, and place the liver slices in the skillet. Cook until the bottom is nice and brown. Turn and cook until the second side is also nice and brown.

6. Add the onions and reduce the heat to medium. Cook a bit longer until the liver is just a bit pink on the inside.

Fire

WHEN MY BIG BROTHER WAS SIX years old he caught on fire. He was just standing and watching Dad help the neighbor burn weeds. Mr. Schuldeis had a can of gasoline to keep the fire going. He threw some on the fire, but a trail of it came back with the can and the fire followed it and went right up Ron's arm, caught his sweater on fire, and his face. He screamed, turned around, and started running. Dad ran after him and caught him. Dad rolled him in the dirt to put out the fire. When he turned him over, the skin on his face was all burned. My father made the huge mistake of taking his cotton-gloved hand and wiping it over Ron's face. All the skin of his face came off on the glove. Ron was in agony and his faced puffed up so much that he could only sip liquid through a straw. When Mom took Ron to see Dr. Lovitt, he put some "goop" all over Ron's face. It looked even worse with the "goop" spread thick all over it. Mom asked the doctor if Ron would be terribly scarred. Dr. Lovitt said they would have to wait until it healed.

Mother was not happy with this vague answer, and she was not happy about the goop. She called her sister Esther and told her the horrible story, and Aunt Esther dropped everything and came to see how bad Ron was. She took one look at him and went back to her farm and gathered a dozen fresh eggs, a coffee can, a little old gas outdoor stove, and a clean feather. She came back and fired up the stove out in the back yard. She separated the yolks from the whites, put them in the clean coffee can, and put the can on the stove. When the yolks had been cooked for about 30 minutes, an amber oil separated from the solid part of the yolk. This was strained through cheesecloth to get all the solid yolk out; a beautiful light egg oil was left. You must cook the eggs outside because the smell is absolutely horrible. The sulfurous odor will knock you down.

Aunt Esther and Mom went to Ron's bedroom and tried to wipe the doctor's heavy salve off his face. He was kicking, screaming, and flailing. Mom sat on him and held his arms down and Aunt Esther wiped his face clean with a warm soft white cloth. Then they applied the egg oil with the feather ever so gently over his face. They did this every day for a week and a half until Ron's face was completely healed. He went back to school in two weeks with no scars and you could not tell his face had been burned. The only telltale sign of the burn is when Ron is out in cold weather and his face will turn red in some areas.

Aunt Esther got this recipe from her mother, Grandma Bauer, who got it from her mother, Great Grandma Eckhardt, who came from Russia. Grandma Bauer used the egg oil on her son Henry when he fell against the wood stove with his hands and burned them very badly. Aunt Esther had watched her make this concoction for her brother and remembered it.

This isn't a food recipe, but rather a fascinating glimpse into folk remedies from the old country.

Let's Have a Picnic

I HAVE A VERY LARGE FAMILY. MY dad was one of seven and my mother was one of eight siblings. Her father, my Grandpa Bauer was one of 12. When a family picnic was planned, it really couldn't just be at someone's home. We had to pick a city park! We would go to the Torrington City Park, Mitchell, NE City Park, or Scottsbluff, NE City Park. There would be between 75 and one hundred family members, and it was all about Grandma Nab. She loved picnics. She would sit, facing outward at a picnic table or in a folding chair, and when one of the families arrived, all the family members must first go and say hello to Grandma Nab. She would hug all the children and comment on how big they were all getting.

Before the picnic, one of the family members had to go to the park on the designated Sunday and save a shelter with tables under it. Everyone else would arrive after changing clothes after church. Every family would bring between two and four items, plus drinks, like big jars of ice tea or lemonade. The tables would groan with German dishes such as cucumber salad, kraut birok, dena kuchen, grebbles, and German chocolate cakes. Of course, there would also be fried chicken, pies, salads galore, and watermelon. My family loved watermelon. Most of my aunts had a specialty food that no one else made because no one else could make it as well. Aunt Esther Wagner made the best grebble and no one else could even come close. Once in awhile, someone else would also bring grebble, but it was always heavy or greasy. We would all try to be polite and eat the "bad" grebble so that the person who made them wouldn't be embarrassed by having them all left in the pan at the end of the picnic. Grebbles are like light doughnuts that are twisted into a figure eight and deep fried, and then rolled in sugar. I could eat six at least! Aunt Esther always made dozens of grebble for the picnics. We would have picnics for Mother's Day or the Fourth of July or Grandma or Grandpa's birthday—any excuse to get together.

The men would play horseshoes. The children would play volleyball or badmitten, or just chase one another and have water fights. Everyone pretty much stayed for lunch and dinner. It would be dark when things were gathered up, dragged to cars, and taken home. There were sunburns, tummy aches, sprained wrists, and great times. I had more cousins to play with than some children had in a class in school.

Here is Aunt Esther Wagner's grebble (doughnut) recipe. It will take practice to become good at this dish. I'm also including cucumber salad, which is my favorite summer salad.

GREBBLE

Serving Size: 4 ounce

Total Servings: 36

   1 cup buttermilk

   1 cup sour cream

   3 beaten eggs

   3 teaspoons baking powder

   1 teaspoon soda

   1/4 cup sugar

   1 teaspoon salt

   4 1/2 cups unsifted flour

1. Mix all the ingredients in the order given. The flour will be added last, and 1 cup at a time. The dough mixes together very easily and is soft and pliable.

2. Chill several hours or overnight.

3. Roll the chilled dough out on a floured board to 1/8-inch thickness. Cut the rolled out dough into 5" squares. Cut a slit in the middle of each piece, pick it up, twist once, and fry in fat until golden brown. Turn only once. It is best to use a deep fryer such as a Fry Baby so that you can set the temperature at 375 degrees. Shortening such as Crisco is the best choice for frying these doughnuts and the shortening when heated should be 3 or 4 inches deep. Let the grebble cool on paper towels to absorb any excess grease after they have been removed from the fryer.

4. Roll in sugar and watch them disappear.

Mother's Tip

Vegetable oil or shortening are good choices for this recipe. Do not overheat the oil or the grebble will fry too fast and burn. Cooking at 375 degrees is just right. If you do not have a deep fryer with a temperature knob, you can use a heavy kettle. When heated on a medium temperature the shortening or oil will start a slow rolling simmer when it has reached 375 degrees.

CUCUMBER SALAD

Serving Size: 6 to 8 ounce

Total Servings: 8

6 medium cucumbers

6 hard-boiled eggs

1 medium onion

1 pint buttermilk

1 teaspoon salt

1 teaspoon pepper

1. Wash the cucumbers, peel them, and thinly slice them crosswise into a large salad bowl.

2. Coarse chop the hard boiled eggs and add them to the cucumbers.

3. Coarse chop the onion and add it to the eggs and cucumbers.

4. Add the salt and pepper.

5. Pour the buttermilk over the salad and stir.

6. Refrigerate for 30 minutes.

7. Serve in salad bowls as a side dish.

Sugar Beet Harvest

IN THE PLATTE RIVER VALLEY, WE raised sugar beets, and in October, if all went well, we pulled them out of the ground with big topping machines and trucked them to a factory to be unloaded and processed into the bags and packets of sugar that you see on the supermarket shelves in the baking aisle.

The topper works like this: It is hooked to a tractor and driven down the row of beets. The machine pulls the beets out of the ground, cuts the big green tops off, dumps the beets into a holding bin, and then a conveyor belts rides them out of the bin and into a truck that is driving alongside the topper. It's pretty tricky to keep the truck under the conveyor, and it's also tricky to know when the truck is full and shut off the conveyor. The whole family had to help with beet harvest. Often, neighbors would help you if you helped them. Uncles would help my dad if he helped them. That was because you needed two trucks, one loaded and driving to the factory, and one being loaded, and we only had one big truck. My brothers drove the trucks along under the conveyor when they became old enough to help, and my dad drove the topper. My mom got the job of driving the loaded truck to the factory, and because at the time of this story, I was too young to go to school, I had to ride in the truck with Mother. I hated it. Dad always loaded the truck so heavy, and he even had extra tall sideboards added on at harvest time so the truck box could hold more. I was always scared of the whole thing. First of all, when we got to the factory, there might be a long line of trucks waiting to unload so we had to wait and wait, and we knew Dad would be getting impatient. Then, Mom had to drive the truck up onto this thing called a piler. A man on the piler would step to the passenger side of the truck, unhook the box and then hook two chains to the box that were attached to a boom. The boom would lift the box on its side so that the sugar beets would slide down and fall into a holding well that had a conveyor belt running through it. The conveyor carried the beets up and dumped them on a big pile. My mom's job was to put the truck in park on the piler and step out on the running board of the truck and jerk the chain loose that held the side of the truck box closed. This time, Mom stepped out of the truck and jerked the chain free. As she did this there was a huge explosion and dirt and debris flew everywhere. I froze, and did not move an inch, but my mother jumped into the pit and the conveyor belt was running toward a covered chute that would crush her. The piler operator was alert. He saw Mom jump, and he turned the thing off. Turns out, Dad overloaded the truck and two of the tires blow out. Everyone in the other trucks had run up to see what had happened. One of them drove the truck off the piler for Mom because she was really shook up, but unhurt, thank goodness. Someone had to go get my dad, and he called the tire store and got them to come to the factory with new tires.

I never liked that piler in the first place. I always felt like the whole truck was going to slide into the pit. After the big explosion, I was scared and didn't want to ride with Mom anymore. I don't know how Mom was brave enough to keep on driving that truck. I suppose she just did not have any choice. Dad loved my mom with a passion and I know he would have preferred that Mom not have to work like a hired man, but there was no money for hired men. Mom was the help he had until Tim and Ron were old enough to help more.

I drove the big truck after harvest was over. After school or on Saturdays, Tim and I were delegated to drive up and down the sugar beet fields and pick up all the loose beets that were left scattered all up and down the rows. The beets couldn't be left lying about because later Dad would buy some cattle and turn them loose in the fields to eat the beet tops that were left in neat wide rows. If a cow found a sugar beet and tried to eat it, she could choke to death.

Tim would put the truck gear in low and leave me to steer to the end of the field. He would walk beside the truck on either side looking for beets, and then jump into the truck and turn it around for me. I almost ran over him once because I couldn't reach the brake pedals, and he was running around the front of the truck to jump in and stop it at the end of the field. He was so mad at me, he made me get out and walk and look for beets while he drove. Actually, I liked walking the fields. It smelled really good, like crushed sweet leaves and rich, loamy soil.

Because this story is all about sugar, I would like to share some wonderful desserts that have been in my family for generations.

APPLE CRISP

Serving Size: 5 ounce

Total Servings: 6

6 large apples peeled, cored, and thinly sliced

1/2 cup granulated sugar

1/2 teaspoon nutmeg or cinnamon

1 cup all purpose flour

1 cup brown sugar

1/2 cup butter

1. Preheat oven to 325 degrees.

2. Grease an 8-inch square baking pan.

3. Spread the apples in the bottom of the pan. Top with granulated sugar and sprinkle nutmeg or cinnamon on top of sugar.

4. Mix the flour and brown sugar.

5. Cut the butter into the flour mixture with your fingers until the mixture resembles coarse meal.

6. Spread over the apples. Bake 1 hour.

7. Serve with ice cream or whipped cream.

Mother's Tip

This is a good dish to make along with baked potatoes and meat loaf.

GINGERBREAD DELUXE

Serving Size: 4 ounce

Total Servings: 9

2 cups sifted flour

3/4 teaspoon salt

2 teaspoon baking powder

1/4 teaspoon baking soda

3/4 teaspoon ginger

3/4 teaspoon cinnamon

1/8 teaspoon cloves

1/2 cup shortening

2/3 cup sugar

2 eggs

2/3 cup molasses

3/4 cup boiling water

1 cup whipped cream

1. Sift together flour, salt, baking powder, baking soda, and spices. Set aside.
2. Cream together the shortening and sugar.
3. Beat in eggs, one at a time.
4. Gradually add molasses, beating constantly.
5. Use the low speed on the mixer to blend in the set aside flour.
6. Add water. Mix until smooth.

7. Pour into well greased and floured 8 or 9 -inch square pan. Bake at 350 degrees for 35 to 45 minutes.

Mother's Tip

This gingerbread is great with homemade whipped cream.

SNICKERDOODLE COOKIES

Serving Size: 2 ounce

Total Servings: 3 dozen

1 cup soft shortening (part butter)

1$1/2$ cups sugar

2 eggs

2$3/4$ cups flour

2 teaspoon cream of tartar

1 teaspoon soda

$1/4$ teaspoon soda

1. Cream the shortening, then add the sugar, and then the eggs.
2. Sift the dry ingredients together, add to the creamed mixture, and stir together.
3. Form dough into balls the size of a walnut and roll in a mixture of 2 tablespoons sugar and 2 teaspoons cinnamon.
4. Place about 2 inches apart on a baking sheet.
5. Bake 8 to 10 minutes at 375 degrees.

One Dead Chicken

THIS STORY GOES BACK BEFORE MY time, but I just have to tell it. This is about my dad when he was a young boy, maybe 11 or 12 years old. Grandma Nab had chickens and geese, and Dad had the job of going to the granary where Grandma had some hens sitting on nests of eggs. She needed some chicks to increase her laying hens. So one morning, he was sent to the granary to take the bushel baskets from over the hens, take them off the nests, give them food and water, and let them run around a little bit. There was one hen that was not at all interested in being caught and put back on the nest with a bushel basket over her head. I don't know how long Dad chased around that elusive hen. I mentioned that my dad had a tempestuous side, and he got very angry with this stubborn old hen. He finally was able to grab her, and he threw her against the wall. Then she was, very, very still. She was dead! Now, Dad was pretty worried because, after all, Grandma had a worse temper than he did, and he knew that he was really in for a hard whipping when she found out what he had done. He thought about this problem for awhile, and then decided to put the hen back on the nest and arrange her just so, so she looked like she had just died sitting there trying to hatch her eggs. The thing that I find astonishing is that he got away with it! Grandma Nab bought into the whole big lie. She felt so sorry for that darned hen and said the poor thing must have just starved herself to death sitting on that nest. Dad never ever told Grandma what really happened because Grandma might have gotten mad even after 40 years.

I've decided that chicken and dumplings would be a good recipe for this story. A nice fresh hen is where you should start!

CHICKEN AND DUMPLINGS

Serving Size: 12 ounce

Total Servings: 6

1 large whole roasting hen

1 medium chopped onion

1 bay leaf

1 1/2 teaspoons salt

Water

2 well beaten eggs

1/4 teaspoon baking powder

Enough flour to make a stiff batter, about 1 cup

1 medium onion

1/2 stick butter

1 cup cream

1. Put the roasting hen in a large pot with the hen covered with water. Bring the water to a boil and then reduce the heat to a simmer.

2. Add chopped onion, a bay leaf, and salt to taste.

3. Simmer until tender, and then remove the hen.

4. Strain the broth through a piece of cheesecloth into a large bowl. Put the broth back into the pot after you have strained all the bits out, and bring the broth to a boil. Add the dumpling batter.

5. To make the dumplings, mix together the eggs, baking powder, and flour. Add the flour a little at a time until you have a stiff batter. You might not need the whole cup of flour.

6. Drop a dime-sized spoonful of batter into the broth and cook covered until the dumplings rise to the top of the kettle. Reduce heat.

7. Add onions, butter, and cream. Two chicken bouillon cubes may be added to the broth for added flavor.

8. Slice the chicken, and serve the dumplings and broth over the chicken.

Take a Break

IN THE SPRING AND SUMMER ON the farm, the men were out in the fields from sunup until sundown. They would be ditching, cultivating, weeding, irrigating, or putting up the alfalfa. My brothers were out in the fields as soon as they could drive a tractor, maybe seven or eight years old.

My job was to help Mom make a midmorning snack and get it out to whichever field they were in. Usually it was fried egg sandwiches on toast, homemade dills, cookies, and iced tea or ice water. Mom and I would get the sandwiches ready and wrap them in waxed paper, along with the cookies or cakes and jars of tea. It all went into a big paper sack, and I had to ride my bicycle to take the food out to Dad and Tim and Ron. The obstacle to all of this was that it was a big sack, and I had no basket on my bike. I usually just rode with one hand on the handlebar until I got tired of holding the bag. Then, I would change hands and ride a little further. Then I would just get tired of the whole thing and ride with both hands holding the bag and no hands on the handlebars. I got pretty good at this, and you know, even my brothers were impressed. It was a mile or two out to the fields, depending on which one I was going to. I always got to share 10AM lunch too, and I was pretty hungry.

I will tell you how Mom made the egg sandwiches before McDonald's got the idea, and Mom's recipe for 14-day crock dill pickles.

FRIED EGG SANDWICHES

Serving Size: 12 ounce

Total Servings: 6

6 eggs

12 slices white bread

1/4 cup butter

1. Heat a big frying pan, and melt a tablespoon of butter in it.

2. When the skillet is medium hot, crack the six eggs into it. Cover and let fry.

3. Meanwhile, toast the bread and butter it.

4. Turn the eggs over one by one and break the yolk in each one. Let them fry about 1 or 2 minutes.

5. Lift each fried egg out, put it on a slice of toast, and cover with another slice of toast.

6. Wrap in wax paper, put the six sandwiches in a paper bag, and take to the fields for lunch. If you can ride your bike fast enough, they will still be warm when you get there.

CROCK DILLS

Serving Size: 4 ounce

Total Servings: 30–36

   30–36 pickles

   4–5 cloves garlic

   10 stalks dill

   1 medium onion

   Brine:

   2 gallons water

   2 cups vinegar

   1 cup salt

1. Place a generous layer (4 or 5 stalks) of dill in the bottom of a 5-gallon crock.

2. Layer 30 to 36 fresh cucumbers fitted closely together on top of the dill. Scatter 3 to 4 cloves of garlic and 1 medium onion among the cucumbers as you layer them.

3. Heat the brine until the salt is dissolved and then bring the brine to a boil. Boil about 1 minute.

4. Pour the brine over the cucumbers and add a second layer of 4 to 5 stalks of dill

5. Cover the dills with a plate turned upside down that fits closely inside the container. Weight it down with a glass quart jar that is filled with water. You don't want the cucumbers to float. The cucumbers will be ready to eat in about 3 days, but they are really good after about 14 days.

Okay, We Have to Talk about Funerals

MY DAUGHTER THINKS MY FAMILY IS morbid. We go to the cemetery quite often to visit our relatives who have passed. We clean the graves and talk to our people who are gone from us. We buy our plots and erect the gravestones before we pass. When I go to visit my mother in Torrington from Phoenix, one of the first things I do is go "visit" Daddy. I talk to him, pull the weeds, and give him some roses. Red roses were his favorite. We have a blurry line drawn between life and death. We remember them, honor them, and talk to them so we can keep them alive in our hearts.

When I was a young child in the 1950s, people didn't go to the hospital to die. They were at home with the whole family coming and going, and the women bathing, cleaning, and feeding them. When they passed, the gathering would begin. Family came to the house with food. Neighbors came by for just a few minutes to drop off a casserole or a cake. The family stayed with the grieving family all day, and someone would often stay the night. You were never alone. There was so much food brought to the house that you could get through a week without cooking. Good food was the way that people could show you that they loved and cared about you. There would be scalloped potatoes, a jello salad, brownies, a ham, a vegetable tray, white cakes, and chocolate cakes. It was endless with wonderful expressions of love.

When I was 15, Grandma Nab passed away at the age of 83. It was 1965, and we were more modern by then. Grandma had cancer and was in the hospital. She wasn't eating much of anything because it all tasted bitter to her. I would go after school and sit with her so that Mom could have a break and maybe run errands. I would just hold her hand and brush the bugs off her arms that she thought were crawling on her. Dad spent a lot of time with her too. Someone was with her all the time because she didn't speak English and couldn't communicate with the nurses and doctors, and we didn't want her to have to pass to heaven alone. It was a very dry year and the crops were not coming up properly. Dad would talk to her about the farm and how much he needed some rain. Grandma said to him in German, "Mein kindt, wenn ich im himmel, ankomme schicke ich dir regen deine ernte" ("My child, when I get to heaven, I will send you rain for the crops").

One evening, the nurse told us we should go home and get some rest. They would call us if anything was wrong. Of course, while we were gone for those few hours Grandma went home to God all by herself. My father was devastated. He was her youngest. He sobbed and sobbed because he would miss her so much. He cried so hard at the funeral that he couldn't get his breath. When the funeral was over, and Grandma's casket was being carried down the steps of the German Congregational Church, a big cloud sailed right over and big drops of rain started to fall on her casket. The big drops turned into a downpour that went on for quite a long while, and was enough to bring Dad's crops up and bring in a bumper harvest in a few months. It rained so much that water ran down the crop rows as though Dad was irrigating. Grandma kept her word about the rain, and let us know she got Home all right. She had a great send off. The church was full. People had to stand in the back as there were no more seats left.

When Grandma Bauer left us, it was a similar big funeral even though she hadn't lived in Scottsbluff for years and years. She was brought from Portland, Oregon, and her funeral was the day before Thanksgiving 1985. Her children came from Portland and Texas and her grandchildren came from all over the United States. She was buried next to Papa Bauer who had passed in 1956. She never remarried. Mom's sister Esther had everyone stay at her house because she had a big house in town with six bedrooms and five bathrooms. It was an interesting group of people. There was sister Katherine who was now Sundari Peruman and a Hindu. She had her husband Markandya with her. There was brother Pete, a Jehovah Witness, and sister Doris and her husband Don. She was considered "normal." Mom's side of the family was very eclectic to say the least, and Grandma Bauer embraced them all. She didn't seem bothered by the diversity. When Mom spoke of her siblings, she always stuck sister or brother to the front of each of their names—brother Hank or sister Mary. I don't know why they did this, but I always found it very endearing. I was known as "Sis" many times throughout my childhood.

Some people might think that this mish mash of people and religions might have made for a horrible few days, but everyone seemed to celebrate differences as something good and exchanged childhood stories and philosophies with aplomb.

Again, the church was packed. Uncle Pete, being a Jehovah Witness, said he couldn't enter the Salem Congregational Church. Mom was very calm, but furious. She said God knows no boundaries, and as he was the only surviving son, he would be in that church right beside her! He was.

This was still a time of an open casket at a funeral. The casket would be put in the foyer of the church and everyone attending the funeral would have to pass the person for one last look. As people passed by they would touch Grandma's hand or face or kiss her cheek or lips. I couldn't do it. I found it appalling. I did take one last look. She was the last of my grandparents, and I felt bereft and lonely. Mom was very stoic. It was almost scary, but she had cried a lot at home, and I think she was empty of tears.

After the funeral, Mom and I decided that something must be done for Thanksgiving, which was the next day. Mom had a turkey that she was going to cook. We drove home that evening after supper with everyone and stayed in her kitchen for hours preparing dinner for the next day for 20 or more people. I made sage dressing and sweet potatoes with brown sugar and butter. Mom got the turkey cleaned and stuffed. We made a couple of pumpkin pies and a Waldorf salad. At around midnight, we collapsed in bed, but Mom set the alarm for four. We got up and put the turkey in to roast and made mashed potatoes. When it was all done, we wrapped everything in tea towels and blankets to keep it hot, put it in the trunk of the car, and Dad drove us 30 miles to Aunt Esther's house. Aunt Esther had the table set beautifully because she had some stunning china and silver. We sat down at one in the afternoon, blessed the food, and ate like truckers. I was awfully tired, but I still had to jump up from dinner and catch a plane back to Phoenix. Of course, half my relatives accompanied me to the little Scottsbluff airport. My family is very emotional, and they like to hold your hand, kiss you, cry, and wave until the little plane is out of sight. I always got great send offs with lots of tears and thank yous. I miss those send offs. Now it's just Mom standing by the window waving and watching my little 12-seat plane race down the runway toward Denver. No one is with her, not Aunt Esther Schmidt or Aunt Esther Wagner or Dad or Aunt Alvina. They are all in the cemetery where I go to lay down a few roses and talk.

This story could have a thousand and one recipes, but I'm going to tell you how to make great scalloped potatoes, ice box cake, strawberry pretzel salad, and German pot roast.

SCALLOPED POTATOES

Serving Size: 8 ounce

Total Servings: 6

6 potatoes, pared and thinly sliced—about 3 cups

1/4 cup minced onion

3 tablespoons butter

2 tablespoons flour

2 teaspoons salt

1/8 teaspoon pepper

13/4 cups milk

1. Place half of potatoes in a greased 11/2 quart casserole dish.

2. Sprinkle half of onions over the potatoes.

3. Melt the butter in a saucepan.

4. Add flour, salt, and pepper to the butter and stir together with a wood spoon.

5. Add the milk to the flour and butter. Stir constantly and bring almost to the boiling point. Remove from the heat and pour half of the mixture over the ingredients in the casserole.

6. Repeat with the remaining potatoes, onion, and sauce. Cover and bake one hour at 350 degrees.

GERMAN BEEF POT ROAST

Serving Size: 12 ounce

Total Servings: 6

3- to 4-pound beef roast, chuck roast, or seven bone roast

2 cups water

1 tablespoon salt

1/2 medium sized onion

4 bay leaves

6 Potatoes

4 large carrots

Pepper to taste

Cabbage (optional)

1. Place the meat in a roaster; salt the meat.
2. Add water, onion, and bay leaves.
3. Cover the roaster and bake in a 300 degree oven for 2 hours.
4. After the 2 hours, add the pepper and peeled potatoes, allowing 1 potato per person,
5. Add the carrots - scraped and cut in half, and then quartered.
6. Add a small amount of water to partially cover the vegetables. Bake, covered, 2 hours at 300 degrees.
7. Uncover the roaster and bake at 375 degrees to brown the potatoes slightly.
8. A head of cabbage, cleaned and quartered may be added when adding the potatoes.

ICE BOX CAKE

Serving Size: 6 ounce

Total Servings: 15

1 cup butter

2 eggs

2 cups whipped cream

1 cup walnuts fine chopped

1 1/2 cups powdered sugar

1 8-ounce can crushed pineapple, drained

1 pound vanilla wafers

1 teaspoon vanilla

Crush wafers and place in the bottom of a buttered 13 x 9-inch glass casserole dish, saving about 1 cup of the wafers for the top of the cake.

1. Spread the pineapple on top of the crushed wafers.

2. Cream the butter, sugar, and eggs thoroughly. Spread the mixture on top of the pineapple.

3. Add the finely chopped walnuts to the whipped cream; flavor with vanilla and a little powdered sugar and spread on top of the butter mixture.

4. Top everything with the remainder of the crushed wafers and chill in the refrigerator for several hours.

STRAWBERRY PRETZEL SALAD

Serving Size: 6 ounce

Total Servings: 15

2 cups finely chopped pretzels

1/2 cup melted butter

8 ounce cream cheese

1 cup powdered sugar

2 cups whipped topping

6 ounce strawberry jello

2 packages frozen strawberries

2 cups boiling water

1. Mix together the pretzels and butter. Pat the mix into a 9 x 13-inch glass pan, and bake at 350 degrees for 10 minutes.

2. Mix together the cream cheese, powdered sugar, and whipped topping.

3. Spread the cream cheese mixture over pretzel mixture, and chill about 1 hour.

4. Dissolve the jello in the 2 cups of boiling water; add the thawed strawberries. Allow it to partially set up in the refrigerator.

5. Pour the jello over the cream cheese and finish setting for 2 hours in the refrigerator.

6. Cut into squares and serve cold.

HAPPY PILLS

I HAD A MOST BELOVED AUNT, SUNDARI Peruman. Her name at birth was Katherine Bauer and she was my mother's older sister. She had lively, smiling eyes and the most infectious laughter, a laugh that made you laugh just to hear it. She was a beautiful woman inside and out. My mother said that she had a perfect hourglass figure.

In the middle of her life, Katherine decided to embrace Hinduism. You can just imagine how a family of Volga German Lutherans felt about such a "heathen" idea! At first everyone was bewildered and then, it was "a phase Kay is going through", then there was anger, but after some years when Aunt Kay stuck to her guns and never wavered from her commitment, the family became accepting of her life and dreams.

Right after Aunt Kay became a convert, she and her daughter Kitty came to the farm from California for a summer visit. Now, Kitty and I are the same age and that summer we were seventeen. She had long wavy blond hair, a bit of a crooked smile, and a big imagination. It was 1967. Kitty and I loved each other immensely, even though we were seldom together. We could stay up half the night telling each other stories and having discussions about boys. We had been relegated to the living room floor because Aunt Kay had to have my bedroom all for herself. She was meditating and practicing yoga exercises and needed "privacy". Kitty and I, and the rest of my family had a few good laughs at Aunt Kay's expense. You have to picture a bunch of down to earth farmers trying to make sense of the "Hindu Thing".

Colors are meaningful and Aunt Kay was wearing white only that summer. She had the most stunning white suits and lingerie that you can imagine. There were gold buttons, pencil skirts, and lace everywhere. Kitty and I were a little jealous. Next to her, the only thing we had going for us was our youth. She was absolutely gorgeous. I think the yoga was really working!

After being on the farm for about a week, Aunt Kay decided that she had a job for Kitty and I. She needed us to make her some organic laxative pills. Oh my god, the howls of laughter from us could have been heard all the way to town. We had to get out the big white Sunbeam mixer and attach the meat grinder to it. Kitty mixed up a concoction of prunes, dates, grains, and vitamins. Then we had to force this mixture through the meat grinder to make into a paste that we could roll into quarter size balls. Smoke rolled out of Mom's mixer just as we were about to finish. It smelled like burning rubber. Kitty and I didn't know whether we should laugh, cry, or just get hysterical. Aunt Kay came into the kitchen when she smelled the smoke. She looked at us and said that we needed to settle down and think "happy thoughts" as we were making these prune balls or they would not would not turn out right and wouldn't help her digestion. From then on, in my family, laxatives became "happy pills". I believe that for the rest of my life, I have never laughed as hard or long as I did that day. The "pills" had to be rolled in powder sugar and stored in a sealed glass container. None of the rest of us ever tried them, and you know, my mother's mixer never did work very well after that day.

Aunt Kay became Sundari Peruman a few years after the "happy pills" incident, a lifelong Hindu, and a vegetarian.

The family came to admire and respect her enormously. She was very well known and respected in the Hindu community. When she died, her ashes were scattered in India, a scholarship was endowed in her name, and there is an eternal flame burning in a temple on the island of Maui to honor her.

When Sundari looked at you, you felt as though she had seen to your core and knew all your secrets, but that it was alright because we are all human and fragile. There was discernment with warmth in her stare.

I adored my Aunt Sundari and I hope she is watching over all of us at this moment and always.

DATE PINWHEEL COOKIES

Serving Size: 2 ounces

Number of Servings: 24

1 cup shortening

1 cup white sugar

1 cup packed brown sugar

3 eggs

4 cups all-purpose flour

½ teaspoon salt

1 teaspoon baking soda

1 teaspoon vanilla extract

2 ½ cups chopped dates

½ cup white sugar

1 cup water

1 cup chopped walnuts

1. Blend together the shortening, 1 cup of white sugar, and the brown sugar. Add the eggs, vanilla, flour, soda, and salt. Mix this very well and set the dough aside.

2. To make the date filling, combine the dates, ½ cup white sugar, water and walnuts. Cook in a heavy saucepan over medium heat until the mixture thickens. Pull it off the stove and cool it. If it is necessary, add water to the filling until it can be spread easily.

3. Divide the dough into 4 parts. Roll out each piece on a floured surface to ½ inch thick. Spread each piece with the cooled filling. Roll the dough up jelly roll style. Pinch

the ends closed and place the rolls on a cookie sheet. Refrigerate until the dough is cold.

4. Slice the chilled rolls ¼ inch thickness and bake at 400 degrees for 10 minutes.

SWEET POTATO AND PRUNE CASSEROLE

Serving Size: 6 ounces

Number of Servings: 8

6 sweet potatoes

1 (16 ounce) jar stewed prunes

¾ cup honey

¾ teaspoon ground cinnamon

1 teaspoon salt

1 ounce prune juice

2 tablespoons lemon juice

¼ cup butter

1. Pierce the sweet potatoes and place them on a greased cookie sheet. Bake the potatoes for 1 hour at 425 degrees, or until they are tender. Cool the sweet potatoes and then cut them into ¼ inch slices.

2. In a small bowl, combine the honey, cinnamon, salt, lemon juice, and prune juice, and melted butter.

3. Cut the prunes in half and remove the pits. In a casserole dish, arrange alternating layers of prunes and potatoes. Spoon the honey mixture over each layer.

4. Bake for 45 minutes in a 350 degree oven. Baste the casserole occasionally with the honey mixture in the casserole.

BANANA AND PRUNE MUFFINS

Serving size: 3 ounces

Number of Servings: 12

½ cup white sugar

¼ cup vegetable oil

1 egg

1 cup mashed banana

½ cups all-purpose flour

1 teaspoon baking powder

½ teaspoon baking soda

¼ teaspoon salt

¼ teaspoon cinnamon

1 cup chopped dates

1. Preheat the oven to 350 degrees and grease and flour a muffin pan, or use the paper liners.

2. In a large bowl, combine the sugar, oil and eggs. Beat this until it is smooth and then add the banana and vanilla. Mix together the flour, baking powder, baking soda, salt, and cinnamon. Stir the flour mix into the egg mixture and stir until it is just moistened. Mix in the prunes and spoon into the muffin cups.

3. Bake in the preheated oven for 20 to 25 minutes or until a toothpick inserted into the center of a muffin comes out clean.

It's All in the Game

I HAVE TO SAY THAT FOR AS long as I can remember, my father loved baseball. Because we lived "way out there" in Wyoming, there was not a major league team in a city near our home. There wasn't even a city near our home! Dad had a choice of a California team, such as the Dodgers or the Angels, or the Cardinals in Saint Louis. He decided that the Cardinals would be his team. This was before I was born, and you know, Dad was a Cardinals fan until his last breath. He said, "Once you chose a team, you had to stick with that decision."

On Saturday afternoons in the mid sixties, major league baseball games were on television, and Dad and I would try to get all our work done so we could watch baseball. I liked baseball too, and of course, I liked the Cardinals because he did, and because they had some crazy good players like Bob Gibson. We would settle in the living room with popcorn, Hershey bars, and Dr Pepper. Of course, Dad was very vocal and believed the "ump" was an idiot and had no eyes, and he thought he could do better if he was the ump. We had a pretty good time, and after it was over, we went back to irrigating the sugar beets or scrubbing the kitchen floor.

After I had married and was living in Phoenix, Mom got Dad to get on a plane to come for a visit. This was no easy task. Dad did not want to fly. He was a little scared and didn't like having someone else in charge of navigation. It was March, and the weather was already hot. It was Spring Training though, and I was so determined to take Dad. We went to see the Chicago Cubs in Scottsdale, and it was 103 degrees. Dad didn't mind in the least. He said the heat felt so very good on his bones. We had pretty good seats up close to the players. Dad was so thrilled to see these guys in real life. He said that they looked so much bigger in person. Dad had never been to any ball games, not even minor leagues. We had hot dogs, popcorn, and peanuts in the shell. I started throwing my peanut shells on the floor between my feet, and my Father had a fit. "What did I think I was doing? You can't make a mess like that. We'll get thrown out!" I had the hardest time convincing Dad that one is supposed to throw the shells on the floor and make a mess that would be cleaned up by sweepers after the game. He was holding his shells in his hand. At that moment, I thought my Dad was the sweetest, nicest man. He never did understand why it would be okay to throw peanut shells all over. Mom taught us all about being neat and clean!

I thought this story should have a good peanut butter pie or peanut clusters or peanut butter cookies in celebration of one of the nicest days my Dad and I had together—just the two of us at the ballpark.

PEANUT BUTTER CREAM PIE

Serving Size: 4 ounce

Total Servings: 6

1 8-ounce package cream cheese

1/4 cup powdered sugar

1/2 cup peanut butter

2 tablespoons milk

8 ounce of Cool Whip topping

1 8-inch baked pie shell

1. Beat the cream cheese and powdered sugar together until light and fluffy.

2. Add the peanut butter and milk to the cream cheese mixture.

3. Add the Cool Whip, and beat the mixture together until it is smooth.

4. Pour into a baked pie shell, and chill for 5 or 6 hours.

5. Garnish with peanuts if you like and serve with lots of whipped cream.

PEANUT CLUSTERS

Serving Size: Each cluster is about 1/2 ounce

Total Servings: Makes 100 peanut clusters

2 packages candy coating found in the baking aisle of any grocery store

4 cans of salted Spanish peanuts

1. Melt the candy coating in the microwave at 1-minute intervals. Stir the coating between the intervals until it is melted.

2. Pour all the peanuts into the candy coating and mix thoroughly.

3. Drop by teaspoons on aluminum foil and let them set firmly. This makes at least 100 clusters.

Mother's Tip

The clusters can be frozen and will keep for 3 months.

PEANUT BUTTER COOKIES

Serving Size: 2 ounce

Total Servings: 4 dozen

1 cup sugar

1 cup butter

1 cup smooth or chunky peanut butter (I prefer smooth)

2 teaspoons soda

A pinch of salt

1 cup brown sugar

2 eggs

2 cups flour

1. Cream sugars and butter together.
2. Beat in the eggs. Stir in the peanut butter.
3. Add the soda, flour, and salt. Mix well.
4. Roll the dough into balls, place them on an ungreased cookie sheet, and flatten them with a fork.
5. Bake in a 400-degree oven for 8 to 10 minutes.

Mother's Tip

You can easily double or triple this recipe with great result. This recipe is good to use as a learning tool for children wanting to learn how to bake.

My son, Ryan, as a small boy, loved to stand on a chair beside me when I was making these cookies and smash the rolled up balls down with a fork. He was very patient as he waited for me to roll them up for him. Any child will have fun doing this and can learn about baking at the same time.

Goin' to the Chapel

REMEMBER GOING TO SUNDAY SCHOOL AND church service every week? Do you remember having no choice in the matter, and what's more we never thought to question our parents or God about whether we had to go or not. If we were not dead or dying Mom took us to Sunday school, went back home, got dressed up, got Dad dressed up, and came back to church to attend Sunday services. We joined them in the sanctuary and then entered church and sat in a row like toy soldiers. For the longest time, I was too young to understand the sermons, but I was also not allowed to fall asleep. I could only look forward to the hymn singing, which I absolutely adored. If we started falling asleep or acting up in any way, Mom would pinch us on the arm. Or, she would say "Wait til you get home." My mom was no slacker. If she said you were going to get it, you did, but "it" was usually just a talking to about respecting God's house.

When I was three years old, and I do not remember this, I was standing between Mom and Dad in the front seat of the car, and we were on our way to church. I have no idea what my Dad said to me, but I told him to shut up. Don't ever tell your Dad to shut up. I think before he even thought, he reacted and slapped me across the mouth. I started crying and couldn't stop, and then I was so upset, I broke out in hives. We didn't make it to church. The hives lasted two weeks, but the good thing was that my dad never ever hit me again. The bad thing was that I was a little scared and nervous around my dad for years and years.

Mom started taking us to the Presbyterian Church when I was two years old. When we started attending, it was just a small white church with a beautiful steeple and was one block off Main Street in Torrington. Just a couple years after that, they built a lovely big brick and stained glass beauty that was up on the hill overlooking Main Street and the valley. It was huge and had the longest aisle to walk down if you were getting married. In fact, Tim and I did get married there.

Our family has always liked going to church, but the miracles have never happened in church. They happened out in the world when we least expected them. There was the time that Aunt Katherine who became Aunt Kay, who became Aunt Katya, who became Sundari Peruman, my mother's sister prayed a car into starting. The Bauer brothers and sisters were all in Portland because Papa Bauer was very sick. Uncle Hank and my mom were visiting Aunt Kay's house because she lived in Portland at that time. Uncle Hank got in the car to leave, and it wouldn't start. Aunt Kay watched for awhile, and then she said "Just a minute Hank, just a minute." She disappeared into her bedroom for a couple of minutes, came out, and said, "Start the car, Hank." He's snickering at her, but turns the key over and the car starts, and not only that, it is purring like a kitten. My mom says, "Sister Kay, you do have a hotline to God!" Mom got in the car with Uncle Hank and they drove off as though a miraculously starting car was not a thing out of the ordinary. When Aunt Kay became a Hindu and changed her name to Sundari, her second sight—seeing beyond the veil—really kicked in. She would call Mom because she knew something was wrong or something was going to happen. She would warn Mom, and Mom always listened. I believe that the women in the Bauer family get this sight or intuition. I have a bit of it, but my daughter Nikki sees and feels the angels. I will tell her if I'm worried about one of us flying or driving on a vacation, and she will say that she feels the person will be fine or that she feels nothing bad. Once, when my son Ryan was traveling to Wyoming twice within a month, I was rather worried and told Nikki so. She said, "Mom, we have sent Ryan so many angels to protect him that they are plastered all over his pickup. There is hardly room for Ryan!" We always pray angels around our family whenever they are traveling.

As for spirits visiting us, we most certainly have a lot of that! My first husband Ron passed away at the young age of 50, and I don't think he wanted to go yet, so he visited everyone quite a lot. His favorite way to let you know he was about was to make pictures fall off the wall. He did this to Nikki so much, and in the middle of the night, that she got up one night and made a trip around the entire house saying to him, "Dad, I know it's you. And I know you love me and I love you too, but you are really scaring us, so please stop knocking things off the walls, and playing with the lights and appliances. I'm fine now and you can go home." He has not touched a single thing in her house since.

My father, Harold, passed on at the age of 87 on March 19, 2007. He hung out at my house for months after that. When I got home to Cave Creek from attending his funeral, my husband was a bit mystified and said that he had found a perfect red rose stuck in our metal tiki torch in our backyard. It had been raining heavily. We could find no footprints, and the little creek that runs when it rains was running full and could hardly be crossed. My husband David put the rose in a glass bowl, and it was perfect and lovely. David said that it had appeared on Friday, and I said, "That was the day of Dad's funeral." We had had a church full of red roses because they were his favorite, and I believe with all my heart that he left me a message of love and hope that day. Dad turned my computer off, and turned lights on. I woke up one night at 3 a.m. and the ceiling fan light was on as bright as day. I hadn't turned it on, and David was sound asleep. Tables have been moved at odd angles, and candles have gone sailing around corners at a 90-degree angle. David is creeped out by all these happenings, but I feel oddly comforted to know Dad wants to be where I am and wondering if he is trying to tell me something. He has departed from my house in the past few months. I did not tell him to go. I feel he was satisfied that I would be all right on my own and passed through the veil for the last time.

Do I have an odd family? Most certainly and I wouldn't have it any other way.

I thought Daddy's favorite meal would be the best recipe I could give you here.

LIVER SAUSAGE

Serving Size: 6 to 8 ounce

Total Servings: 36 sausages

1 cleaned pig's head

1 pig heart and 1 pig tongue

1 pork liver

1 10-pound pork roast

3 tablespoons salt and

2 tablespoons pepper

Sausage casings

1. Clean a pig's head.
2. In a large kettle boil the head, heart, tongue, and 1 lean pork roast until it is very tender.
3. Pull the membranes off the heart and tongue. Pull the meat off the head.
4. Have 1 pork liver boiling in a separate kettle.
5. Grind all these meats together, and then season with salt and pepper.
6. Stuff the meat into clean casings. Casings are pig intestines that are cleaned thoroughly and soaked in salt water overnight. Tie these shut and boil them until the sausages rise to the top of the kettle.
7. Remove and cool.

Mother's Tip

1. This sausage tastes a lot better than it sounds. We would

have it for breakfast or supper with soft-boiled eggs and toast.

2. Daddy loved to have fried liver sausage, a couple of three minute soft boiled eggs, and some of Mom's cherry dena kuchen or cherry bread.

3. To clean a pig's head you will have to clean the cavity of the brain matter. You can ask your butcher to get the pig's head for you and to clean it also. Today, as we don't do our own farming and butchering, we rely on our butcher to fulfill odd requests such as this one.

Your Wedding Will Last Three Days

$\mathcal{B}$Y THE TIME I HAD DECIDED to get married in 1970, three-day Dutch hop weddings were a rarity, but 20 to 30 years earlier, it was quite common among the Volga Germans. A young man asked his beautiful lady to marry him, and if she said yes, he then had to ask her father for permission to marry her. If both families were in agreement, the planning could begin. The bride and grooms' families were both involved in the wedding plans because the wedding and reception would last for three days and there was a lot to prepare. After the church ceremony, which was almost always in the Lutheran Church, the wedding reception was held in a big hall. My mother said that the American Legion Hall in Minatare, NE was usually the choice. The groom's family would have to butcher a steer or a hog or both. Several women would be asked to cook for the three days. It was considered a great honor to be one of the cooks at these weddings because it meant you were a very good cook. Both my Grandma Nab and Grandma Bauer were frequently asked to cook. The first day of the wedding was always noodles and butterballs. The second day was light rye bread and garlic sausage, and the third day was big pots of vegetable beef soup. Of course, there were loads of other salads and desserts to go with these meals. There were kegs and kegs of beer and endless bottles of whiskey. Whiskey was very cheap at that time. There would be a polka band with a dulcimer. The drinking, eating, and dancing began right away and lasted all through the night until three or four in the morning. Wedding revelers would be arriving home to fall in bed when the other farmers were going out to work. Quite a few of the guests never got home. They were a bit under the weather, so they would just sleep on the chairs, benches, or in their cars. At around 10 in the morning, the party would begin again! If you wanted to have a dance with the bride, you had to pin some money on her wedding gown. If there was a particular song you wanted to dance to, you had to give the band some money. Some of the wealthy old

German farmers would pin $100 on the bride's gown for a dance. The more they drank, the more they liked to brag and show off. The bride had to wear her gown for the whole three days. I was told that her dress would just be in tatters all around the bottom from the fast polka dancing and some clumsy men. The bridesmaids would cut off all the tatters so the bride could keep on dancing. If the bride got too tired to go on or just needed a break, it was the bridesmaids' job to stand in for her. On the third day, the exhausted cooks were called out of the kitchen to rounds of applause. A hat was passed for them and was overflowing with money when it reached them. The band played a song for them and they all danced, with wild abandon. They brought out all the glasses, plates, or bowls that had cracked or chipped and smashed them on the floor as they danced round and round with their aprons billowing out.

People always complained about having to go to these Dutch hop weddings, but really they loved it. They could see people from all over the Platte Valley. They could eat and drink all they could hold, and they would have heard enough gossip to last them at least six months. People felt as though they had had a real party, and they were exhausted and satisfied. The food was the best that you would find anywhere. I have my Grandma Bauer's recipe here for German garlic sausage, and Grandma Nab's recipe for rye bread through her daughter, my Aunt Esther Wagner. Both recipes came from Russia.

I can't imagine getting married for three days, but somehow, I feel I might have missed out on some great moments. I mean, if it took three days to get married, you would feel like you had really gotten married! Many of the old ways are getting lost as we scatter to the four winds. The tradition of a three-day wedding is lost to us, except through the memories of our old ones. My mother was my source for this story. I could literally see her reliving these times as she told me about these weddings. My mother and her sisters did not have Dutch hop weddings, but they attended many of them when they were young girls or had been chosen as bridesmaids.

GERMAN GARLIC SAUSAGE

Serving Size: 8 ounce

Total Servings: 60 sausages

20 pound pork

10 pound ground beef

1 cup salt

1 cup pepper

5 or 6 garlic cloves

1/2 cup hot water

Casings for 60 sausages, purchased at the butcher shop

1. Wash and dry your hands and arms thoroughly before beginning.

2. Through a meat grinder, grind 30 pound of sausage meat in proportion of 2/3 pork sausage to 1/3 ground beef.

3. Mix in a stainless steel tub with 1 cup of salt and pepper to taste.

4. Crush 5 or 6 cloves of garlic. Add about ½ cup hot water to the crushed garlic; let steep about 1 hour. Strain and add the liquid to the meat.

5. Mix the sausage meat thoroughly with your hands.

6. Fry a patty to flavor test before stuffing into clean washed casings.

LIGHT RYE BREAD

Serving Size: 3 ounce

Total Servings: 50 slices (10 slices per loaf)

3 cups light rye flour

1 cup white flour

1/2 cup sugar

5 cups water

2 packages dry yeast

1 tablespoon salt

1/4 cup corn oil

7 to 8 cups white flour to be added later

1. Dissolve the yeast in 1/2 cup warm water and 1 tablespoon sugar.

2. Add remaining ingredients, except the white flour, to make a sponge. Cover, and let rise about 1 hour.

3. Stiffen the dough with 7–8 cups white flour.

4. Knead well. Let rise 1 hour.

5. Punch down. Let rise 1 hour more.

6. Grease 4–5 loaf pans. Divide the dough into loaves, and put into pans.

7. Let rise 1 hour and then bake 50 minutes at 400 degrees.

The Little Hellion

Ron, **MY OLDEST BROTHER, WAS AN** only child until he was six years old. Needless to say, he was a handful and was surrounded by adults for companions. Mom says she spent a lot of time on her knees praying to God to help her get him grown up.

Ron could somehow slip away from everyone in the blink of an eye. Dad found him in the hog pen once surrounded by these huge pigs. They were as big as he was, and he was about 3 years old. They got his hat and started to eat it, but my Dad rescued him and his hat. Ron loved that little straw hat and wouldn't give it up. He wore it anyway, tatters and all.

On another occasion, Mom and Dad were visiting at Aunt Esther and Uncle Charlie's house, which was pretty close to highway 26 in Scottsbluff, NE. There were other people visiting that Sunday; all of a sudden there was a knock at the door, and there stood a soldier with Ron in his arms. He asked if this little boy belonged here because he was out walking down the road. Luckily, the soldier was hitchhiking home, scooped Ron up, and probably saved his life. This would have been around 1944 or 45, so there were a lot of soldiers out and about. After that, Mom had had it and she and Dad fashioned a harness out of leather and rope and just tied him up to a clothesline pole so that they could keep track of him.

That is just the tip of the iceberg. When he was maybe two or three, he was crawling around under the kitchen table at Aunt Esther's house. Mom and Aunt Esther were visiting and having a cup of coffee. The coffee pot was always on at Aunt Esther's house. Ron sees how nice Aunt Esther's calf looks, and he crawls over and just takes a big bite. After Aunt Esther got over the shock and screeching, she politely crawled under the table with Ron, took his leg and bit him back! Ron howled, but he found a new respect for

Aunt Esther that day. He never challenged her again, and she never had to bite him again.

I saved the best story for last. Aunt Esther, Uncle Charlie, a hired man named George Dorsch, Mom, Dad, and Ron were sitting down to supper at Aunt Esther's house. Ron was in his little high chair and the food was on the table. Mom had made a plate of mashed potatoes, gravy, and peas for Ronnie (as he was called then). Uncle Charlie was sitting across from Ron, and the devil was in Carl that evening. He said, "Hey, Ronnie watch!" And he rubbed his hands together and then he pretended to pat his hands flat into his own mashed potatoes and gravy. Then, he pretended to rub his hands all over his head, which wouldn't have mattered, because he was pretty bald. You know what comes next. Ronnie patted his hands into his gravy and peas and really did rub great globs of it into his red curly hair. Uncle Charlie laughed so hard that he had to leave the table. Aunt Esther is yelling "Chaarrlie!" My Mom is sitting there just stunned and staring. Dad just about fell out of his chair from laughing so hard. Of course, the men could laugh all they wanted because they didn't have to clean Ronnie up!

It sounds like I'm picking on my big brother, but I'm not. I just think he was the most interesting of the three children. Tim and I were very dull next to Ron.

Ron actually did reach adulthood, married a wonderful lady, Loretta, my sister-in-law, and had three very accomplished children of his own. He knows that I love him with a passion, but his stories just beg to be told.

Since my brother was such a little "devil" throughout childhood, I thought the devil's food cake recipe was just right.

RED DEVIL'S FOOD CAKE

Serving Size: 6 ounce

Total Servings: 10

1/2 cup shortening

13/4 cups sugar

1 teaspoon vanilla

3 eggs, separated

21/2 cups sifted cake flour

1/2 cup cocoa

11/2 teaspoons soda

1 teaspoon salt

11/3 cups cold water

1. Cream shortening and 1 cup of the sugar until light in color and fluffy looking.

2. Add the vanilla and egg yolks, one at a time, beating well after each addition.

3. Sift together the dry ingredients; add to the creamed mixture alternately with the cold water, beating after each addition.

4. Beat the egg whites until soft peaks form; gradually add 34 cup sugar to the whites, beating until stiff peaks form.

5. Fold into the batter; blend well.

6. Bake in two greased and lightly floured nine 11/2 -inch round pans at 350 degrees for 30 to 35 minutes.

SOUR CREAM FROSTING

1 6-ounce package semi-sweet chocolate pieces

1/4 cup butter

1/2 cup dairy sour cream

1 teaspoon vanilla

2 1/2 to 2 3/4 cups confectioners' sugar

1. Melt the chocolate pieces and butter over hot, not boiling, water (double boiler).

2. Remove from hot water and blend in sour cream, vanilla, and 1/4 teaspoon of salt.

3. Gradually add enough confectioners' sugar for a spreading consistency; beat well.

4. This recipe will frost the top and sides of two 9-inch layers or one 10-inch tube cake.

Helen the Housekeeper

E ALL REMEMBER OUR FIRST PAYING job don't we? Mine was as a teacher's helper at a country school. There were five kindergarten children and I was in charge of teaching them to count and read and tell time. This was in a two room school that was forty miles from a town.

My mother, Helen answered an ad in the Scottsbluff Star Herald for a housekeeper as her first job. She was fifteen years old and needed money to help her family survive. Although she was living with "Mama" and "Papa", there was just not enough money to take care of a large family.

Helen became a live in housekeeper for Doctor Wyrens, his wife, and three sons. She lived with them Monday through Friday and earned 3 dollars a week. It was 1937. Mother said that she liked this job very much. The Wyrens family treated her as though she were part of their family, even having her sit down and have meals with them. She did not have to do laundry or cook. The laundry was sent out and Mrs. Wyrens did the cooking with mother's help. Mrs Wyrens made pot roast, meat loaf, spaghetti – things that Mom had not had to eat. The Wyen's house was a big two story with the bedrooms on the second floor, including Mom's.

Mother's job was to dust, mop, sweep, scrub floors, make beds, wash dishes, and set the table. At this house Mother discovered how modern, well to do people lived. They had nice china for meals, and liner, and silver, and they used them every day. They had beautiful manners and discussed books and school and politics. Doctor Wyrens sometimes spoke about a particularly difficult patient. It was so different from the German spoken at her house and the endless talk about farming, animals, canning, butchering, or where the next dollar would be coming from. Mother kept all of these things in the back of her mind. She knew that she wanted to be more American.

After about two years with the Wyrens, Papa Bauer decided to move to a little farm in Torrington, Wy. Mother had to move with them, but she immediately applied for another housekeeping job that was available with Sheriff DeWitt and his wife in Torrington. Once again, she became a beloved part of the family, and was given the privilege of dining with the family. The sheriff and his wife had one daughter, but she was married and living in northern Wyoming. Mom only had to keep house for two people. She said that is was an easy and enjoyable time.

Lots of Mother's friends and cousins also worked as housekeepers. The wealthy families who could afford live in help only wanted to hire the German girls. They were so hard working and so clean. They were reliable and did not steal. Since there was such a large community of Volga Germans in the Platte River Valley, it was easy to hire a German girl to keep the house spotless.

Mother worked for Sheriff DeWitt until she was eighteen and married my father, Harold. She had promised to marry him if he would wait until she was of age. He had asked to get married when she was only sixteen, but she said no to that. She thought that was way too young and she was right.

Mother's two jobs as a housekeeper were invaluable to her in the years ahead. She found out about American ways and foods, and when she had a family of her own to care for, she cooked some American foods, made us all speak English only, and joined the Presbyterian Church in Torrington instead of the German Congregational Church. Mother wanted to fit in and she wanted her children to be wholly American.

Helen served us some great German meals, but she also made a lot of modern dishes. She and I sat down one summer and wrote down as many of these meals as we could remember. We had no recipes and had to make educated guesses as to measures. These are scattered throughout the book and are easy, inexpensive meals from the fifties and sixties.

CHEESY HAMBURGER CUPS

Serving Size: 8 ounce

Total Servings: 6

1 pound lean ground beef

2 tablespoons brown sugar

1 tube refrigerated biscuits

¾ cup shredded cheddar cheese

1/2 cup barbecue sauce

1/4 cup chopped onion

1. Preheat the oven to 350 degrees.

2. Brown the ground beef with the onions and drain.

3. Add the barbecue sauce and brown sugar to the hamburger and onion.

4. Separate the biscuits and place each biscuit in an ungreased muffin cup. Press the biscuit dough up the sides of the muffin cups.

5. Spoon some of the meat mixture into each cup.

6. Bake in the 350 degree oven for 10 to 15 minutes, until the biscuits are brown.

7. Sprinkle the cheddar cheese on top of the meat and return the cups to the oven for 5 more minutes until the cheese has melted.

8. Makes 10 to 12 cheesy hamburger cups.

STUFFED PEPPERS

Serving Size: 1 filled pepper

Total Servings: 4

4 green bell peppers

2 cups cooked white rice

1 1/8 teaspoon salt

2 8-ounce cans tomato sauce

1 pound ground beef

1/4 cup chopped onion

1/8 teaspoon pepper

1. Cut off the tops of the peppers and remove the seeds. Rinse the peppers to remove all the seeds. Set these aside.

2. Combine the beef, rice, onion, salt, pepper and 1/2 can of the tomato sauce. Mix together with your hands or a spatula.

3. Spoon the hamburger mixture into the green peppers and place into an oven safe baking dish.

4. Pour the remaining tomato sauce over the peppers.

5. Cover the dish tightly and bake at 350 degrees for 1 1/4 hours.

6. Baste with the tomato sauce in the bottom of the dish twice.

PUMPKIN POT

Serving Size: 8 ounce

Total Servings: 6

1 7-pound pumpkin

1 1/2 pound garlic sausage

1 cup sliced sweet pepper

1 1/2 cups chopped onion

2 apples, cored and cubed

2/3 cup dry white wine

1/2 cup water

1/3 cup raisins

1 teaspoon sugar

1/4 teaspoon dried thyme

1. Preheat the oven to 350 degrees.
2. Cut the top off the pumpkin and scoop out the seeds and stringy pulp.
3. Place the pumpkin, cut side down, in a 13 x 9 x 2-inch baking pan.
4. Fill the pan with water to a depth of 1 inch. Bake the pumpkin for 1 1/2 hours.
5. After the pumpkin has been baking for 1 hour, prepare the filling.
6. Cook the sausage in a large skillet over medium high heat.
7. Remove the sausage and add the peppers, onions, apples to the skillet. Sauté until the onions are transparent.

8. Add the wine, water. Raisins. Sugar, thyme, and cooked sausage. Simmer for 20 minutes.

9. Take the pumpkin from the oven and discard the water.

10. Replace the pumpkin, cut side up, in the pan.

11. Fill the pumpkin with the sausage mixture, mounding at the top if necessary.

12. Cover the top with foil and return to the oven to bake for 10 minutes.

13. Serve this dish directly from the pumpkin, scooping out some pumpkin flesh to accompany each serving.

CASSEROLE BAKED POTATOES

Serving Size: 6 ounce

Total Servings: 6

6 medium sized potatoes

1/2 cup butter

1 cup crushed saltine crackers

Salt

Pepper

1. Peel the potatoes and rinse them clean.
2. Melt the butter in a small saucepan on low heat.
3. Roll the potatoes in the butter in the saucepan and then roll them in the cracker crumbs.
4. Place the potatoes side by side in a casserole dish and sprinkle with salt and pepper.
5. Bake in a 400 degree oven for 1 hour.

Loretta May and Lorraine Marie

UP A HILL AND OVER A small rise and off to the right is a small white one story house. It is well cared for and surrounded by a fence and a grassy yard. It is just off Sugar Factory Road in Scottsbluff, Nebraska and it was once the home of my Aunt Mary Shaneman, my mother's older sister, and Uncle Reuben. They were newlyweds and it was the early 1930's. Uncle Reuben was a musician who liked a pretty woman and a good drink. He was also a tall, handsome man who played the accordion beautifully. There were dancehalls scattered throughout the valley, so that he was kept very busy with wedding, birthdays, etc. Why Aunt Mary married Uncle Reuben was a mystery to everyone because she wasn't keen on drinking or his eye for a pretty girl. Aunt Mary was only sixteen when she got married, and she went to all of Uncle Reuben's musical engagements just to keep an eye on him. Naturally, after a short time, she was expecting and couldn't follow Uncle Reuben around so much.

When it came time for the birth of her baby, the doctor and Grandma Bauer went to the house to help Aunt Mary. Women had their babies at home during the depression years because there was not enough money for a hospital stay, which at that time, was for ten days. Aunt Mary did well and didn't labor too long. To the doctor's surprise, she had twins, little identical girls, who were way too small. The doctor did not expect them to live. They were so small that they could fit in the palm of your hand. They were so small that Grandma Bauer made them each a crib out of a woman's shoebox and lined them with fluffy cotton batting so that they would feel safe and comfortable. They were so small that Grandma had to use handkerchiefs for diapers. They were too small to breast feed so Grandma Bauer had to buy a goat and have my mother Helen, who was about 10 years old at the time, learn to milk it. My mother trained the goat to jump up onto a table at milking time to make it easier for herself. She named that goat Annie. The little girls were fed with an eye dropper until they grew big enough for a bottle.

Everyone worked very hard to save the twins. Someone was with them at all times. The twins should not have lived, but I believe that Grandma Bauer and Aunt Mary saved them. They were baptized and named Loretta May and Lorraine Marie. They grew and became such dainty, exquisite children. Grandma took care of them quite often because Aunt Mary felt she had to be with Uncle Reuben. They would drop the twins off and be on their way to some engagement. Grandma was very particular that Aunt Mary's house be snug and warm before she would send them back. When the twins were fourteen months old, and walking and chattering away, they were taken from this world so fast it would make your head swim, It was snowy and cold, in the middle of a long winter, when the trips between houses was too much for their fragile lungs. They caught double pneumonia and died within three days of one another. This was so heartbreaking to the whole family that no one really speaks about the twins to this day. The family put heart and soul into saving them, fell in love with them, and lost them, within such a short span of time.

Loretta and Lorraine are buried at one end of the grave of my mother's baby brother Henry. There is a small marker to show where they are, and Mother and I still put flowers out for them on special occasions.

There is only one picture of the twins in our photo album. They are lying in a tiny white coffin, together, and looking like an actual pair of angels.

ANGEL FOOD CAKE

Serving Size: 8 ounces

Total Servings: 8

1 cup sifted cake flour

3/4 cup sugar

12 egg whites

11/2 teaspoons cream of tartar

1/4 teaspoon salt

1 1/2 teaspoons vanilla

3/4 sugar

1. Sift the flour and 3/4 cup sugar four times.

2. Beat the egg whites with cream of tartar, salt, and vanilla with an electric mixer on high until the mixture is stiff enough for soft peaks to form. The mixture will still be moist and glossy looking.

3. Add the remaining 3/4 cup sugar, 2 tablespoons at a time, continuing to beat with the electric mixer until the mixture holds stiff peaks.

4. Sift 1/4 cup of the flour mixture over the egg white mixture and gently fold the flour in.

5. Fold in the rest of the flour mixture 1/4 cup at a time.

6. Scoop the finished mix into an ungreased 10-tube pan and bake in a 375 degree oven for 35 to 40 minutes. Remove from the oven.

7. Invert the tube pan and let the cake cool completely before removing it from the pan.

Under the Trees

JOHN AND SUSANNA, MY GRANDPARENTS, LIVED under a huge canopy of Chinese Elm trees. It was wonderfully cool and shady to sit under them on a hot August afternoon. Mom and I would visit at least once a week, usually on Saturday, before we went grocery shopping.

Grandpa, who was a small, thin man with a slight stoop, had one acre of grass, and trees, and neatly laid out flower gardens. The flower garden was laid out in perfect, straight rows that were easy to irrigate. There was a path beside each row He would walk me down the little paths between the flowers, and tell me the flowers' names and point out their progress from one week to the next. When we walked together, I noticed that he smelled faintly of the rich, fresh earth, and the Prince Albert tobacco that he used to roll his own cigarettes. Now, as an adult looking back, I can see that Grandpa seemed sad and beaten down by life, and all that had happened to him, but as a child, all I knew was that I just adored walking among the flowers with him, and climbing the crab apple tree that was at one end of the lawn. It had a nice big Y very low, close enough to the ground for a little person to get a leg up. I would sit in the tree and watch the clouds or listen to the grown-ups visiting and catching up on what all the rest of the family was up to.

After we had visited for about a half an hour my pleasingly plump, good to hug Grandma would go inside their little house and slice up a watermelon and some homemade rye bread. She would put on a long sleeved smock that buttoned up the front to protect the flowered house dresses that she would wear. The most humorous thing about the smocks is that they were outrageous patterns and colors and clashed horribly with whatever dress she was wearing. The wild colors however, always set off her soft snow white hair that when loosened for brushing was almost to her waist. She would bring the melon out and set it on an old rickety wooden table. We would all gather round and take a slice of watermelon and salt it and start munching away. Juice would run down our arms and drip down our chins. It was so delicious. Grandma always had a slice of rye bread with her melon.

Sometimes Grandma would tell us that the currant bushes were ready, and give me a bucket to fill, to take home and make jelly. She had red and black currant bushes that were in rows around the root cellar and she would help me strip the berries from the bushes. She would eat a few, and I would eat a few, and although she had no teeth, she managed to eat as well as the rest of us. We always made jelly, never jam, and the black currants were sweeter and needed less sugar when cooking.

It was so peaceful under those trees. It was like living in a tree house on the ground and the trees were there to protect and shelter. They gave everything a soft, light green glow.

Summer under the trees for me as a child was just magical, and I never realized that Grandpa's house was in a very poor part of town and rather shabby until I was a grownup and drove to the little house to take a picture. But the reality of the shabbiness will never take hold in my mind's eye. It will always be a fairy like kingdom set in a magical grove of trees.

WATERMELON-CUCUMBER SALAD

Serving size: 6 ounces

Total servings: 12

6 cups cubed seeded watermelon

4 cups cubed cucumber

3/4 teaspoon salt

1 tablespoon sugar (optional)

Just under 1/2 cup balsamic vinegar

1. Place the watermelon and cucumber in a large bowl, and gently toss with the salt and sugar.

2. Drizzle with the balsamic vinegar and toss to coat.

3. Refrigerate for 1 hour, then gently toss one more time before serving.

RED CURRANT JELLY

Serving size: 1 teaspoon per slice of toast

Total Servings: 12-14 six ounce jelly jars

4 pound fresh red currants

1 cup water

7 cups white sugar

4 fluid ounce liquid fruit pectin

1. Place the currants into a large pot, and crush with a potato masher. Pour in 1 cup of water, and bring to a boil. Simmer for 10 minutes.

2. Strain the fruit through a cheese cloth, and measure out 5 cups of the juice.

3. Pour the juice into a large saucepan, and stir in the sugar. Bring to a rapid boil over high heat, and stir in the liquid pectin immediately. Return to a full rolling boil, and allow to boil for 30 seconds.

4. Remove from heat and skim off the top foam.

5. Ladle or pour into sterile 1/2-pint jars, filling to within 1/2-inch of the top. Wipe the rims with a clean damp cloth.

6. Melt the paraffin wax in a double boiler over medium heat.

7. Pour melted paraffin wax on top of the jelly after the jelly has cooled somewhat. Make sure the paraffin is poured on enough to seal the edges.

8. Put the lids on and store in a cool.

A Family Story of the Herbel Family Cousins

THIS STORY STARTS MANY YEARS AGO, as far back as 1764.

Catherine the Great, a German princess ruling in Russia, issued an enticing colonization proclamation. She said that any German person consenting to settle in Russia would be given a piece of land and would be promised freedom of worship and freedom from taxation. They would have self rule, use their own German language, and have freedom from military service.

This proclamation was posted on a door of a small church in Hesse, Germany, and came to the attention of some German farmers whose crops had failed for six years, and whose homes had been destroyed by war for seven years. Frederick, David and Amalia's father, Reinhardt Quindt's great-grandfather, migrated to Russia at this time. They left Germany and walked to the Baltic sea, the port of Lubeck, and sailed down the Volga River to Saint Petersburg. Henceforth, they were called the Volga Deutsch. They formed their community, which was about 50 miles by 100 miles in size and called their town Dreispitz, which means three corners. The town was four miles from the Volga River. They spent many happy years here and enjoyed prosperity and freedom greater than they had ever hoped for. They would not have returned to Germany had they been given the opportunity. Reinhardt Herbel and Amalia Quindt, my father and mother, lived in the area of Dreispitz, Russia.

Gottfried Herbel and Julia Bush, Reinhardt's mother and father, had seven children. Their names were Gottfried, David, Marie, Alex, Reinhardt, George, and Victor.

Reinhardt Quindt and Anna Elizabeth Steinle, Amalia's mother and father, had ten children. Their names were Reinhardt, Anna Elizabeth, David, Gottfried, Frederick, Amalia, Andrew, Alexander, Jacob and Amelia.

Reinhardt was born May 6, 1900. Amalia was born February 7, 1901. Both families grew and prospered. The people were very resourceful and self-sufficient. Their standard of living came from hard work and ingenuity. They lived on large farms and raised their own produce, such as potatoes, cabbage, beets, and carrots. They had a large orchard with apple and cherry trees. They also grew wheat and corn, which was made into flour for their homemade bread. Their homes included fireplaces and ovens for baking. The rooms were large. The beds were placed along the wall and were shoved into each other. They had straw mattresses and feather beds. They were aired out in the morning before the beds were made. The meals were eaten in the same room and a large fireplace was used for cooking.

They had a blacksmith shop with large bellows which they used to heat and mold iron. They made their own bricks from peat. They also had a summer kitchen and storage cellars to preserve their fruits and vegetables. They had cows and oxen which they used to plow the land. Horses, chickens, ducks, and geese completed the picture. It was a beautiful, picturesque place with a stream running through that was dammed to create a pond. They had a water wheel that was used to power a flour mill. Life was very good.

Reinhardt and Amalia went to school in Dreispitz, which was about five miles from their home. Whereas, they lived on the outskirts of town, the school was in town. The school master substituted as a part time pastor. The church was next to the school. In the cold of winter the church was not heated, so services were held in the school, which was heated every day. The pastor of this Lutheran church had five churches to serve. Consequently, the school master preached on the Sundays that the pastor was at another church. The children were taught in German, but they also had a Russian class. Each morning they said the Lord's Prayer and a pledge of allegiance to Russia.. The school went to sixth grade, which was equivalent to our eighth grade.

Amalia's brothers, David and Frederick, came to America in 1913. She had always been a favorite of theirs, so with much love they sent her two rolls of ribbon, one pink and one blue. She was so pleased to wear them on her dresses and in her hair. Everyone asked where she had gotten them, and she was so proud to day, "My brothers sent it to me from America." They also sent $10 American money, which was worth $20 in Russia. They sent their father a pair of grey striped slacks and a pocket watch with a chain, and a pair of slacks for an older brother.

Amalia and Reinhardt were married February 19, 1919. On the day of the wedding, they went to Dobrinka and were married. Amalia wore her brother Reinhardt's wife's dress. It was satin and there was no longer any satin available. Musicians were hired from another town. They changed into their wedding attire at a friend's house that was near to the church. After the ceremony, the musicians led the horses, which were decorated with colored paper, roses and streamers, through Dreispitz. They returned to the friend's house, changed their clothes and were toasted as a bride and groom. From there, they returned home where a feast was to be served. A calf had been killed and roasts with potatoes and carrots made. There was homemade chicken noodle soup and lots of coffee cakes (kuchen). The party lasted for three days. Many people from far away stayed overnight. Others who lived nearby left and returned the next day.

When Reinhardt and Amalia moved to the Herbel home, they took along a cow, a horse, and many ducks and chickens. It was like a dowry from Amalia's parents. Amalia had a chifforobe of clothes that were especially nice. One day she came home to see her mother-in-law showing them to her sister. She felt that her privacy had been invaded and asked Reinhardt why they were doing this. He said that his mother was proud to be able to show her sister such pretty clothes.

From even a young age Reinhardt was always doing business from buying and selling oxen, or cows, horses, and grain. In this manner he made his living. His father had died in 1918 at the age of fifty six, just a year before Reinhardt married Amalia, and he had taken over as head of his father's household. The land at that time belonged to the boys. Girls could not own any land. The more boys you had, the more land you received from the Russian government.

Then came the War of 1914. The Bolshevicks took possession

of the country. Everything that was good was gone. The power hungry Bolshevicks rode their horses into the yards and demanded everything. They took it all—the crops in the cold cellars and all the food supplies that had been so hard earned. The Bolshevicks would point their guns at the people and demand even the shoes on their feet. The people were helpless. They had to give what was wanted or be shot. There was no chance for survival under these circumstances. Meetings were arranged in the town and it was decided that the whole village of 192 people would leave on December 4, 1921. They feared for their lives, so they had to leave in the dark of the night so as not to be seen. They left Dreispitz with Amalia's brother Gottfried driving the sleigh which carried Grandma Herbel, Amalia, and Amalia's baby David, just sixteen months old. The sleigh was pulled by oxen that had been hidden from the soldiers. It held their meager food and clothes supplies and any possessions they could carry. They did have work permits to work in other towns, which they needed for travel and which also served as passports. They drove the sleigh to a town about thirty five miles away called "Kamyshin". From there, they started a month-long train trip to Minsk, during which time; the train was sidetracked many times, sometimes for as long as three days. The people were loaded onto box cars that had no heat except for a small fire in the middle of the car. They had gunny bags of money with which they could buy nothing. It was worthless. Material things became what counted, which was proven as they left Minsk to walk to the Polish border.

Many people on the train became sick and could no longer stand the pace. Grandma and Grandpa Quindt and a brother and sister turned back. Nothing was ever heard from them again. Reinhardt and Amalia kept going. While in Germany, Amalia got a letter from her brother, to whom she had written. He said the folks never got back to their home.

While the train was sidetracked, Reinhardt and his sister looked for a place to relieve themselves, and came upon another boxcar. They opened it, and saw that it was full of dead bodies. On top of the pile was a newborn baby. They left at once, and felt no need for a bathroom after what they saw. Many people had measles, and before long, little baby David became ill and died. Amalia wrapped him in a blanket after he died, in hopes of burying him when the train stopped, but the soldiers took him away from them. It was only the beginning of the pain and suffering they would go through.

After leaving the train in Minsk, Reinhardt and Amalia walked and walked. They came across a Jewish man who said he had a goat shed that they could use to get out of the bitter cold. The next day he would lead them to the Polish border. Amalia had on a scarf that he much admired.

The scarf would have been worth one million rubles. This scarf took all the people to the border as a payment for his help.

Amalia loved to crochet and do handiwork. When they left home she was wearing a petticoat with crocheting on the bottom. On their journey, they had no thread, so she would unravel as much thread as was needed to mend and patch their clothes. On walking into Poland, Reinhardt had a knapsack in the front and back draped over his shoulders. He was so exhausted that he dropped to his knees. He just couldn't take any more. Gottfried Steinle and Gottfried Meier lifted him, one under each arm and pumped him up and down to get his circulation going again. At the Polish border, it was early morning with snow falling and the suns shining. Dear God, the people of Poland came out of their houses, which were the size of a one car garage, and waved handkerchiefs and white cloths to welcome them. There, they were taken to barracks, in which they had to live until they were out of quarantine. The people had lost a lot of weight on the trip and were practically starved. Reinhardt and Amalia were in Barracks Number ten until Amalia's feet became so swollen, she was put in Barracks Number 20 for medical help. It was in the barracks that Grandma Herbel and brother George died – more pain and more heartaches. Amalia's feet were swollen from frost, and this unbearable situation was such that she could barely walk, until one day while in Barracks twenty, she found out that Reinhardt and his brother, Alex and Victor, had been shipped to Germany. She also found out that the last train for Germany was leaving. It was her only chance to be reunited with Reinhardt again. A young man who also wanted to get to Germany took her hand and said, "You can make it. Come, let's go. I will help you". They didn't walk, they ran, and they did make the train.

On arriving in Germany, Amalia was scared. A Red Cross worker took her in his arms and said, "Furchte dich nicht; du bist in Vaterland". ("Have no fear, you are in the Fatherland.")

The Red Cross workers took her to a barracks and gave her shoes and a change of clothes – her first change of clothes in a month.

After Reinhardt and Amalia were reunited, they worked in the barracks kitchen peeling potatoes and stirring foods. Here they stayed for six months until they could become German citizens. There was an open quota to the United States for German citizens, but not for Russians. The place they were staying was Frankfurt an der Oder. After they obtained German citizenship, they left for America from the large shipping port of Bremen on the S.S. Hanover.

The Hanover held about five hundred people and the sea journey lasted about twelve days. On the way, a storm developed, and the ship was almost lying on its side. Many of the people were very sick and prayed that the storm would end.

The group from Dreispitz arrived at Ellis Island where they had to go through a physical examination. It was here that Amalia found out that she was expecting little Emma. They left Ellis Island on a small boat for New York City, always wearing a tag with their names and destination, as the ways and language of America were strange to them. Once in New York City, they were put on a bus to the train station, and then onto a train that would take them to Kansas. When they were on the train, they were given a banana, but didn't know what to do with it, so they threw it out the window.

Amalia and Reinhardt arrived in Herrington, Kansas at midnight on August 25, 1922. It was dark and they were very hungry. It was desolate. There were no sidewalks and no pavement, only mud roads. At the railroad station there were watermelons laying on the ground waiting to be shipped. Someone in the group said, "What I wouldn't give to take just one", but Amalia said, "No, or we'll end up back where we came from". A sheriff eventually came along and escorted them to Gottfried and Anna Herbel's house, which was a few blocks from the station. Gottfried was Reinhardt's brother and had put up $435 voucher money for Reinhardt to guarantee that he was not destitute when entering the U.S.. This was to be paid back in hard labor.

There was no big welcome. They knocked at the door and someone hollered, "Come in, there's a bed in the other room." They were so tired, scared, hungry, and disappointed. Their only thought was, "God help us!"

Gottfried (Fred) had a house and two smaller houses on the farm. They were given the house in the front, which was the size of a garage. The house had no electricity, no water, and no bathroom. The water had to be carried into the house for cooking, bathing, and laundry.

Reinhardt had to work on the farm, but also worked for the railroad. One of Reinhardt's jobs was to milk the cows, which were three miles away from the house. He walked this every day and still had to pay ten cents a quart for the milk for his family. Rent for the house was six dollars a month. Amalia took in two boarders who each paid $25 a month. She also did the cleaning, cooking, and laundry for Fred and Anna after they dismissed their maid. Reinhardt and Amalia worked from morning until night everyday for seven months until the $435 voucher money was repaid.

Feeling that they had been taken advantage of, Reinhardt moved his family to Milwaukee and eventually opened a grocery and meat market. They prospered once they had the grocery and Reinhardt was able to retire in 1965.

I thank Irene Herbel Schroder for telling her story for us in a book that I was able to obtain at a Bauer (my mother's maiden name) family reunion in 1993. Their story is but one of the thousands from the Volga Germans flight from Russia.

My grandparents, John and Susanna Nab, also departed for America from Bremen, Germany, but in November 1912. They sailed on the Kronprinzessin Cecilie and arrived at Ellis Island on December 3, 1912. They took the train to Colorado instead of Kansas. They had three of their children with them – Emil, aged six, Marie, aged 3, and Waldemar, aged one year and six months. Johannes (John) was age thirty one and so was Susanna.

The following recipes came from Russia with my Grandmothers. We don't use most of these recipes anymore, but I believe they are of great value historically.

VA RENYA
(Cherries for hot tea)

Serving Size: 1 teaspoon

Total Servings: 60

1 quart cherries with pits

1 quart sugar

Juice of 1 lemon

1. Mix all ingredients and cook. When the mixture comes to a full boil, turn down the heat and boil slowly for 8 to 10 minutes, until it is nice and syrupy.

2. Turn off the heat and put the cherries in jars and seal. Seal the jars using canning jars that have lids with rings.

3. This recipe makes 2 pints.

4. You will need 1 teaspoon of the cherry mixture for 1 cup of hot tea.

EIN GEMACHTEN APFEL

Serving Size: 8 ounces

Total Servings: 40

3 gallons water

3/4 ounce stick cinnamon

1 ounce star anise

4 bay leaves

1/2 pound licorice sweet wood sticks, mashed with a hammer

40 yellow delicious apples

1. Fill a 5-gallon stone crock with perfect yellow delicious apples in layers to within 4 inches of the top.

2. Mix together the water, cinnamon, anise, bay leaves, and licorice in a heavy kettle. Heat the mixture to boiling, remove from the heat and cool. Pour the cold brine over the apples.

3. Put a round wooden board, which fits into the crock, on top of the apples and weight it down with a quart jar filled with water. This is so the apples cannot float.

4. Let the apples stand at cellar temperature for 1 month.

EIN GEMACHTEN ARBUS

Serving Size : 8 to 12 ounces

Total Servings: 100

    50-gallon wooden barrel

    40 small white watermelons

    30 gallons water

    10 cups non-iodized salt

    Cherry and apple leaves

1. Place small white watermelons (King or Queen variety) in the barrel.

2. Thirty-five watermelons will fill the barrel. Take the 5 remaining melons, cut them open, scoop out the melon and distribute the cut up melon throughout the barrel of whole melons.

3. Place a lot of cherry and apple leaves throughout the barrel and over the top of the melons. Fill the barrel with a solution of 1 cup non-iodized salt to 3 gallons of water.

4. Put a weight on the top of the melons such as a rock to keep them from floating.

5. The melons will be ready in about 5 weeks.

3 DAY CROCK DILLS

Serving Size: 8 ounce

Total Servings: 20

20 cucumbers medium length

1 clove garlic

3 dill heads

Solution of 1/2 cup salt to 3 quarts water to cover cucumbers

1. Wash the cucumbers and put them in a 5-gallon crock.

2. Add the garlic and dill among the cucumbers. Heat the solution and pour it over the cucumbers.

3. Put a plate upside down on top of the pickles and weight it down with a quart jar filled with water.

4. Let the cucumbers stand for 3 days and then you can use them straight out of the crock.

Mother's Tip

Mom made these several times during the summer. They are very crisp and refreshing. These dill pickles are good with any sandwich. They are also wonderful in potato or pasta salad.

SAUERKRAUT

Serving Size: 1 quart

Total Servings: 8 servings per quart

1 quart cabbage cut up fine

1 tablespoon salt

1 tablespoon sugar

1. Add salt and sugar to cabbage.
2. Pack the cabbage solid to about 1 -inch from the top of the jar.
3. Add boiling water to fill the jar.
4. Seal the jars with Kerr lids that have been in boiling water. Let stand for 4 weeks.

WATERMELON HONEY (HONICH)

Serving Size: 1 ounce

Total Servings: 60

15 ripe watermelons

Cheesecloth

10 6-ounce jelly jars

1. Take the pulp out of the ripe watermelons, put it into a colander or sieve that has been placed over a large bowl that has been lined with cheesecloth; press out all of the juice with a wooden spoon or pestle. Gently lift the cheesecloth out of the bowl so that any seeds are strained out of the watermelon juice.

2. Put the juice into a heavy kettle and boil to a full rolling boil until it is thick and turns a reddish brown color. When the syrup coats a spoon, it is done.

3. Remove from the heat and pour into jars and seal. You don't need to seal it with wax.

Mother's Tip

This honey can be used for pancakes or a topping for cakes or even poured on a little toast.

HOMEMADE LYE SOAP

Serving Size: 1 bar of soap, about 8 ounce

Total Servings: 25 bars

11 cups cold water

9 cups fat, rendered

1/2 cup ammonia

1/4 cup borax

1 8-ounce can of lye

1. Mix the above ingredients.
2. Add 1 can of lye and stir for 30 minutes. Stir until it is like fudge.
3. Pour the soap into a very large oblong pan and let it set overnight.
4. Cut into bars and store in a cool dry place.

Mother's Tip

When I was very young, maybe 4 or 5 years old, I do remember going out to the barn with mother to make lye soap. I know she built a fire outside and had a large kettle over it that she filled with fat chunks and grease. She had to render the fat and grease, and my job was to stir it. I also remember that she had big deep baker's pans that she poured the liquid soap into, and she let it harden for a few days. Then she would cut it into big square chunks. She would throw a chunk of it into the wringer washing machine to clean the clothes. We also had to use it for bathing. We had no indoor bathroom; we had a large oval tin bathtub and had to lug hot water down to the basement to fill it. We used to make jokes about Mother's soap taking the skin right off of us. We were definitely squeaky clean.

FROZEN CUCUMBER SLICES

Serving Size: 6 ounce

Total Servings: 8

2 quarts thinly sliced unpeeled cucumbers

1 large onion, diced

2 tablespoons salt

1 1/2 cups sugar

1/2 cup cider vinegar

1. Place the onion, cucumbers, and salt in a large bowl, and cover with cold water. Let this stand for 2 hours, then drain.

2. Mix the sugar with the vinegar; pour over the cucumbers. Mix this thoroughly.

3. Pour into pint freezer containers, leaving 1/4 inch head space. Freeze.

4. Thaw the cucumbers by placing them in the refrigerator for a few hours.

CHOKECHERRY JELLY

Serving Size: 1 tablespoon

Total Servings: 120

    5 cups chokecherry juice

    1 package Pectin Sure Jell

    1/2 cup lemon juice

    8 1/2 cups sugar

1. Mix the chokecherry juice, lemon juice, and pectin.
2. Let the mixture boil for 3 minutes.
3. Add the sugar and cook until the juice drops heavy from a spoon. This should be about 8 to 10 minutes.
4. Pour into sterilized jelly jars and seal with paraffin.

Mother's Tip

To obtain 5 cups of choke cherry juice, cook 1 1/2 gallons of chokecherries in a large heavy kettle. Cover the chokecherries with water, bring to a boil, lower the heat, and simmer for 5 to 8 minutes. Strain the chokecherries through a cheesecloth to obtain the juice. This recipe is good for any sour berry such as boysenberries or gooseberries.

Sweet Escapes

I HAVE ALWAYS LIKED MAKING DESSERTS MORE than any other food, so I've decided to finish this little book with a repertoire of my most used and favorite recipes starting with desserts first.

TOFFEE SNACKING CAKE

Serving Size: 4 ounce

Total Servings: 9

  2 cups all purpose flour

  1/2 teaspoon baking powder

  1/2 teaspoon baking soda

  1/4 teaspoon salt

  1/2 stick unsalted butter at room temperature

  2/3 cup sugar

  2 large egg whites

  1 teaspoon vanilla extract

  6-ounce container of plain yogurt (any kind), thinned with a tablespoon of water. Low fat yogurt may be used

  1/4 cup English toffee pieces

  11/2 cups frozen nondairy whipped topping thawed

1. Heat oven to 350 degrees. Coat a 9 x 9 x 2-inch square baking pan with butter and a dusting of flour.

2. In a bowl, whisk together flour, baking powder, baking soda, and salt. Set aside.

3. In a large mixing bowl, beat butter until smooth and fluffy, about 2 minutes.

4. Beat in the egg whites one at a time, and then add the vanilla.

5. With a mixer on low speed, slowly mix flour into the butter mixture until it is smooth.

6. Add the toffee pieces to the mixture and stir in with a wood spoon.

7. Scrape into the prepared pan and smooth out the top. Bake about 25 minutes.

8. Let the cake cool about 10 minutes in the pan. Invert the cake, removing the pan, and let cool 10 more minutes.

9. Cover with whipped topping and sprinkle with cinnamon. Serve or refrigerate until served.

HOLIDAY SHORTBREAD COOKIES

Serving Size: 2 ounce

Total Servings: 24

1 cup butter

1/2 cup confectioner's sugar

1/4 cup cornstarch

11/2 cups flour

1. Preheat the oven to 375 degrees.

2. Whip the butter with a mixer until fluffy.

3. Stir in the sugar, cornstarch, and flour. Beat on low for 1 minute, and then beat on high for 3 to 4 minutes.

4. Drop the cookies by teaspoonful 2 -inches apart on an ungreased cookie sheet. Bake 12 to 18 minutes.

5. Do not let the edges brown too much. Cool on a wire rack. Decorate as desired.

CHOCOLATE TOFFEE

Serving Size: 1 ounce

Total Servings: 20

1 cup finely chopped pecans

1/2 cup butter

3/4 cup brown sugar

1 6-ounce package semi-sweet chocolate chips

1. Spread the nuts over the bottom of an 8-inch square pan.

2. Combine the butter and brown sugar in a saucepan.

3. Bring to a boil and boil for 7 minutes, stirring constantly.

4. Pour the butter and brown sugar mixture over the nuts and let stand for a few minutes.

5. Spread the chocolate chips over the candy. Cover the pan with aluminum foil to keep in the heat.

6. When the chocolate is soft (about 5 minutes), spread it evenly over the candy.

7. Wait 15 minutes and cut the candy into 20 pieces.

8. Store in the freezer or refrigerator.

COFFEECAKE (DENA KUCHEN)

Serving Size: 6 ounce

Total Servings: 24

1 box sweet hot roll mix

Caramel topping (recipe below)

Rival crumbs (recipe below)

1. To make this coffeecake, start with making sweet dough from scratch (using the same recipe as used for the cabbage buns) or from sweet hot roll mix in a box.

2. Make the crumbs (rival) for the topping.

3. When using sweet dough for the coffeecake, roll the dough 1/4 inch thick to fit a 9 x 13-inch pan. Place the dough in the well-greased pan.

4. Let the dough raise about 1 hour in a warm place.

5. Spread the caramel topping over the top of the sweet dough.

6. Sprinkle rival on the top of the filling. You can sprinkle some granulated sugar over the rival.

7. Bake in a preheated oven. Bake the bread at 400 degrees for 10 minutes and then turn the oven back to 350 degrees and bake for another 20 minutes.

RIVAL FOR THE TOPPING

2 cups flour

1$1/2$ cups sugar

1$1/2$ sticks of soft butter or margarine

1 egg yolk

1. Mix the flour, sugar, and butter with your hands. Mix well, and add the egg yolk.

2. Mix until crumbly. Sprinkle on top of the filling when it is ready. If you do not use it all, it can be kept refrigerated for a long time if it is sealed tightly.

CARAMEL TOPPING

1 cup brown sugar

2 cups warm water

1 teaspoon cinnamon

3 tablespoons cornstarch

3/4 cup butter

1. Put 1 cup of sugar in a skillet on medium and brown it. Watch carefully so it doesn't get too brown.

2. When the sugar is all light brown, add 2 cups of warm water and cook until all the sugar crystals are melted.

3. Add 1 teaspoon of cinnamon.

4. Put 3 level tablespoons of cornstarch and some water in a small container. Make a paste, and add it to the burnt sugar. Cook all of this until it is clear and a little thick.

5. Take the sauce off the fire and add the 3/4 cup of butter. If it gets too thick, add a little sweet cream until you get the right consistency.

6. When cool, spread on top of the sweet dough. Then put the rival on top and bake.

Mothers Tips

Canned pie filling of any kind may be used instead of the caramel topping. Blueberry, cherry, or apple are good choices.

ICE BOX DESSERT

Serving Size: 4 ounce

Total Servings: 8

1 cup milk

1 pound marshmallows

2 boxes frozen strawberries

1 cup walnuts

1 cup whipped cream

1 box vanilla wafers crushed

1. Line an 8 x 8-inch cake pan with half of the vanilla wafers. Set aside.

2. Heat milk in a double boiler. Melt marshmallows in milk. The marshmallows will melt quickly in the hot milk; stir gently until the marshmallows are completely melted.

3. Add drained strawberries and nuts.

4. Add the whipped cream to the mixture and stir in.

5. Spread on top of wafers in the cake pan and sprinkle the rest of the wafers over the top.

6. Refrigerate.

Mother's Tip

Drained crushed pineapple or fresh sugared strawberries can be substituted for the frozen strawberries.

This recipe came from my Aunt Mary Schwartz, who was my father's oldest sister.

EASY MIX COOKIES

Serving Size: 2 ounce

Total Servings: 36 cookies

 2 cups butter softened

 1 cup sugar

 4 cups flour

1. Mix the butter and sugar until well blended.

2. Stir in the flour.

3. Roll, shape, or cut any way you like into 2 inch pieces. You can roll the dough out to 1/8 inch thickness and use cookie cutters, or you can roll the dough out to 1/8 inch and then roll the dough up like a newspaper and cut slices of 1/8 inch thickness.

4. Place on an ungreased cookie sheet and bake at 350 degrees for 10 to 14 minutes or until browned. Cool on cookie sheets for 5 minutes. Remove the cookies and cool on wire racks.

5. This makes about 3 dozen cookies and can be halved or doubled.

Mother's Tip

To turn these into Jam Thumbprints, shape the basic dough into 1-inch balls and flatten slightly. Indent the centers slightly with your thumb and again bake in a 350 degree oven for 10 to 14 minutes. When the cookies have cooled, fill the center with a favorite jam or jelly.

With just three ingredients and your imagination, you can create a delicious variety of holiday cookies.

ZUCCHINI BARS

Serving Size: 4 ounce

Total Servings: 30 bars

3 eggs

1 cup canola oil

2 cups sugar

2 1/2 cups flour

1 teaspoon salt

1/4 teaspoon baking powder

2 teaspoons baking soda

1 teaspoon vanilla

2 cups shredded zucchini

3/4 cup chopped dates

1/2 cup walnuts

1. Cream 3 eggs, oil, and sugar.
2. Combine the flour, salt, baking powder, and baking soda.
3. Mix all of this together and add the vanilla, zucchini, dates, and walnuts.
4. Mix well and pour into a greased and floured 12 x 18-inch cookie sheet. Bake at 350 degrees for 25 minutes.
5. Cool and frost.

FROSTING

3 ounce softened cream cheese

1 teaspoon vanilla

2 1/2 cups powdered sugar

Enough milk to make smooth

1. Mix the ingredients together until very smooth.

2. Spread onto the zucchini bars.

GINGERBREAD

1/2 cup shortening

1/2 cup sugar

1 egg

1/2 cup light molasses

11/2 cups sifted all purpose flour

3/4 teaspoon salt

3/4 teaspoon baking soda

1/2 teaspoon ginger

1/2 teaspoon cinnamon

1/2 cup boiling water

1. Put the shortening in a medium sized bowl and stir it until it is soft.

2. Gradually add the sugar to the shortening, creaming it at a low speed with an electric mixer, until it is fluffy.

3. Add the egg and molasses to the mixture and beat at medium speed with the mixer until it is mixed together thoroughly.

4. Sift together in a separate bowl the flour, baking soda, salt, ginger, and cinnamon.

5. Add the sifted dry ingredients to the molasses mixture alternately with the boiling water. Stir after each addition of water and flour mixture using a large wooden spoon.

6. Bake in a well greases 8 x 8 x 2-inch square pan in a 350 degree oven for 35 to 40 minutes.

7. Serve the gingerbread warm with lots of fresh whipped cream.

PUMPKIN BREAD

Serving Size: 4 ounce
Total Servings: 10 slices

1/3 cup shortening

11/3 cups sugar

2 eggs

1 cup canned pumpkin

1 teaspoon soda, dissolved in

1/3 cup cold water

12/3 cup flour

1/2 teaspoon cinnamon

1/4 teaspoon ground cloves

3/4 teaspoon salt

1/4 teaspoon baking powder

1/2 cup chopped walnuts (optional)

1. Cream the shortening, sugar, and eggs until fluffy.
2. Add the pumpkin and soda that has been dissolved in water.
3. Sift all the dry ingredients together, and stir into the pumpkin mixture.
4. Pour into a greased 9 x 5 x 3-inch loaf pan.
5. Sprinkle the chopped nuts over the batter.
6. Bake in a preheated oven at 325 degrees for 60 to 70 minutes.

Mother's Tip

The nuts may be stirred into the batter or omitted entirely.

DATE PINWHEEL COOKIES

Serving Size: 2 ounce

Total Servings: 24 cookies

1 pound dates cut fine

1 cup nuts

1/2 cup sugar

1/2 cup water

1 cup shortening

2 cups brown sugar

1 teaspoon vanilla

3 eggs

1 teaspoon baking soda

1 teaspoon baking powder

1/2 teaspoon salt

4 cups flour

1. Cook the dates, water, and sugar until thick. Add the nuts.

2. Cream the shortening and sugar.

3. Add the vanilla and eggs to the shortening.

4. Sift together baking soda, salt, baking powder, and 2 cups of flour. Add it to the shortening mixture.

5. Add the remaining 2 cups of the flour slowly and mix to a soft dough. Roll out on a floured board, spread with the date mixture, and roll up as for a jelly roll.

6. Chill overnight or at least 4 hours.

7. Slice 1/4 inch thick cookies and bake at 350 degrees for 8 minutes.

STIR CRAZY CAKE

Serving Size: 4–6 ounce

Total Servings: 12

2 1/2 cups flour

1 1/2 cups sugar

1/2 cup cocoa

2 teaspoons baking soda

1/2 teaspoon salt

2/3 cup cooking oil

2 tablespoons vinegar

1 tablespoon vanilla

2 cups cold coffee

1/4 cup sugar

1/2 teaspoon cinnamon

1. Put flour, 1 1/2 cups sugar, cocoa, baking soda, and salt into an ungreased 9 x 3-inch metal baking pan. Stir with a fork to mix.

2. Make three wells in the flour mixture. Pour cooking oil in one well, vinegar in one, and vanilla in one.

3. Pour cold coffee over all the ingredients and stir with a fork until well mixed. Do not beat.

4. Combine remaining sugar and cinnamon; sprinkle over the batter.

5. Bake in a 350 degree oven for 35 to 40 minutes.

__Mother's Tip__

This is an old cowboy chuck wagon recipe that I have used for decades. People absolutely adore it because it has everything – cinnamon, coffee, and chocolate.

LEMON BARS

Serving Size: 2 ounce

Total Servings: 12-15

1/2 cup butter

1/4 cup powdered sugar

1 cup flour

2 eggs

1 cup sugar

2 tablespoons flour

1/2 teaspoon baking powder

2 tablespoons lemon juice

1. Mix together the butter, powdered sugar and flour.

2. Pat down flat into a 9 x 9-inch pan.

3. While this is baking at 350 degrees for 10 to 12 minutes, stir together the eggs, flour, baking powder, and lemon juice.

4. Beat with an electric mixer until it is light and fluffy.

5. Pour the lemon mixture over the baked crust that has been cooling and spread to the edges.

6. Put back in the oven and bake 25 minutes more at 350 degrees.

CHOCOLATE CHINESE NOODLES

Serving Size: 2 ounce

Total Servings: 30

    1 12-ounce bag chocolate chips

    1 12-ounce bag butterscotch chips

    1 10-ounce bag Chinese noodles

    1 12-ounce can cashews

1. Melt the chocolate and butterscotch chips in a glass bowl in the microwave. Use 30 second increments so the chips don't burn.

2. Add the Chinese noodles and cashews. Mix well.

3. Drop by teaspoon onto waxed paper. Let cool until hardened.

4. Makes about 30 cookies. You should probably double this recipe because they will disappear by handfuls.

LIME COOLER BARS

Serving Size: 3 ounce

Total Servings: 36

2$1/2$ cups flour, divided

1/2 cup powdered sugar

3/4 cup cold butter

4 eggs

1/3 cup lime juice

1/2 teaspoon baking powder

1. Combine in a bowl, 2 cups flour and the powdered sugar; cut the butter into this mixture until it resembles coarse crumbs.

2. Pat this down into a greased 9 x 13-inch pan and bake at 350 degrees for 20 minutes or until lightly browned.

3. In another bowl whisk eggs, sugar, and lime juice until frothy.

4. Combine the baking powder and remaining flour; stir into the egg mixture.

5. Pour over the hot crust.

6. Bake 20 to 25 minutes until golden brown.

7. Cool. Dust with powdered sugar and cut into squares. Makes about 3 dozen.

BAKED RICE PUDDING

Serving Size: 5 ounce

Total Servings: 8

    2 quarts milk

    1 cup sugar

    1 cup rice

    Pinch of salt

    1 teaspoon vanilla

1. Place all ingredients in an oven safe baking dish.
2. Place in a 325 degree oven for 3 hours, stirring twice during baking time.

BREAD PUDDING

Serving Size: 4 ounce

Total Servings: 12

1/2 cup butter

2 tablespoon sugar

3 eggs slightly beaten

1/4 teaspoon salt

1 teaspoon vanilla

1/2 cup sugar

1 quart milk

31/2 cups of 1/2-inch bread cubes, white or whole wheat

1. Melt the butter.
2. Combine the butter with the eggs, salt, vanilla, sugar, and milk.
3. Stir until the sugar is dissolved, and pour over the bread cubes.
4. Pour into a 9-inch square baking pan.
5. Bake at 375 degrees for 45 to 50 minutes.

STIR AND DROP CHOCOLATE COOKIES

Serving Size: 2 ounce

Total Servings: 24

> 2 eggs
>
> 2/3 cup vegetable oil
>
> 1 teaspoon vanilla
>
> 3/4 cup sugar
>
> 1 3/4 cups sifted flour
>
> 1/2 teaspoon soda
>
> 1/2 teaspoon salt
>
> 2 1-ounce squares unsweetened chocolate
>
> 1/2 cup finely chopped nuts

1. Heat the oven to 375 degrees.
2. Beat the eggs until well blended; stir in oil and vanilla.
3. Blend in sugar until the mixture thickens.
4. Mix together flour, soda, and salt in a separate bowl. Add to the egg mixture.
5. Melt the unsweetened chocolate in a heavy saucepan on low heat.
6. Add melted and cooled chocolate and nuts to the cookie mixture and stir in until the chocolate is completely stirred in.
7. Drop by teaspoon 2 inches apart on an ungreased cookie sheet.
8. Flatten each cookie with the bottom of a glass dipped in sugar.

9. Bake for 8 to 10 minutes.

__Mother's Tip__

I don't add the nuts to this recipe. I think they are smoother and better tasting without.

UNBAKED FUDGE COOKIE

Serving Size: 2 ounce

Total Servings: 50 cookies

2 cups sugar

1/2 cup butter

1/2 cup milk

2 cups oatmeal

1 6-ounce package chocolate chips

1/2 cup coconut

1. Put the sugar, butter, and milk into a saucepan and bring to a boil.

2. Take off the stove and add 2 cups of oatmeal, 1 6-ounce package of chocolate chips, and 1/2 cup of coconut.

3. Mix well and drop by teaspoon on waxed paper. This makes 50 cookies.

ICE BOX CAKE

Serving Size: 4 ounce

Total Servings: 12

1 box vanilla wafers crushed with a rolling pin

1 16-ounce can crushed pineapple

1 cup chopped walnuts

1 8-ounce or 12-ounce carton of whipped cream

1. Line the bottom of a 13 x 9-inch cake pan with half of crushed vanilla wafers.

2. Spread the crushed pineapple on top of the wafers.

3. Spread the walnuts over the pineapple.

4. Spread the whipped topping over the walnuts with a spatula.

5. Spread the rest of the vanilla wafers on top of the whipped cream, and keep chilled in the refrigerator until you wish to serve it.

MOUNDS CANDY

Serving Size: 1 ounce

Total Servings: 50 candies

1 pound coconut

1 can sweetened condensed milk

1 pound semi-sweet chocolate pieces

1/4 pound paraffin

3 cups chopped pecans

1. Mix the coconut, pecans, and sweetened condensed milk in a large bowl.
2. Chill for 30 minutes.
3. Shape into small walnut-sized balls.
4. Melt the chocolate and paraffin in a double boiler.
5. Dip the balls into the melted chocolate and place on waxed paper to cool.

Mother's Tip

I have found that a potato masher works well for the dipping, and I usually dip them twice. This is a time-consuming project, but well worth it.

PEACH REFRIGERATOR DESSERT

Serving Size: 4 ounce

Total Servings: 10

2 cups shortbread cookies crushed

1 cup heavy cream

2 teaspoons sugar

1/4 cup chopped pecans

1 teaspoon vanilla

2 cups chopped fresh peaches (or 2 packages frozen peaches thawed, drained, and chopped)

1. Sprinkle 1 cup of the cookie crumbs on the bottom of a rectangular 8 x 11-inch baking dish.
2. Whip the cream to stiff peaks.
3. Stir in the vanilla and sugar.
4. Fold in the peaches and pecans.
5. Pour over the crumbs in the dish, and use the remaining cup of crumbs as topping.
6. Cover with waxed paper and refrigerate overnight.

GRANDMA BLANCHE'S CUSTARD

Serving Size: 4 ounce

Total Servings: 12

4 cups milk

1/2 cup sugar

11/2 teaspoons vanilla

4 whole eggs plus 1 egg yolk

Pinch of salt

2 teaspoons nutmeg

1. Heat the milk to scalding and remove it from the stove.
2. Put the sugar in the milk and stir.
3. Beat the eggs slightly and then add gradually to the milk. Add the vanilla and salt.
4. Butter a 9 x 13-inch casserole dish, put the mix into it, and sprinkle nutmeg on top.
5. Place in a shallow pan of water in the oven and bake at 375 degrees until firm, about 40 to 50 minutes.

FRESH RHUBARB PIE

Serving Size: 6 ounce

Total Servings: 6

1 1/3 cups sugar

1/3 cup flour

1/8 teaspoon salt

4 cups rhubarb cut into 1/2-inch pieces

2 tablespoons butter

1. Combine sugar, flour, and salt; add to the rhubarb.
2. Place in a 9-inch pastry dish, and dot with butter.
3. Bake in a 425-degree oven for 40 to 50 minutes.

BULK PIE CRUST

Total Servings: This recipe will make 8 single pie crusts

3 cups shortening or lard

8 cups flour

2 teaspoon salt

1/2 cup sugar

1/2 cup powdered milk

2 teaspoons baking powder

Mix all ingredients very lightly and put into a glass jar or can. Store the mix in a cool, dry place.

Single Crust:

1 1/3 cups mix

3 tablespoons cold water

Double Crust:

2 1/4 cups mix

1/3 cup cold water

Mother's Tip

When you need to make a pie, put the ingredients for a single or double pie in a medium size bowl and sprinkle the water over them. Work the cold water into the ingredients with your hands until you can form a ball the size of a baseball. Place the ball of dough onto a floured surface and roll it out until it is one and a half times the size of the pie pan. Gently pick up the crust by folding it in half and lifting it out of the flour. Place the dough in the middle of the pan and unfold it. Turn under the edges of the crust and pinch the turned under edges between thumb and index finger going all around the edge of the pie pan. Use a fork and prick the bottom and sides of the pie dough so that it does not bubble up when baked in the oven. Follow the directions for baking the pie from the recipe you are using.

COCONUT PIE

Serving Size: 6 ounce

Total Servings: 6

1 1/2 cups sugar

1 stick butter, melted

3 eggs

1 tablespoon vinegar

1 teaspoon vanilla

1 cup coconut plus 1/4 cup coconut

1 unbaked 9-inch pie shell

2 cups whipped cream

1. Mix all the ingredients except the whipped cream and 1/4 cup of coconut, and pour into the pie shell.

2. Bake at 325 degrees for 1 hour.

3. Spread the whipped cream on top of the pie after it has cooled, and sprinkle coconut on top of the whipped cream.

CHOCOLATE CHIFFON PIE

Serving Size: 6 ounce

Total Servings: 6

4 egg yolks

1/2 cup sugar

1/2 teaspoon salt

1 teaspoon vanilla

1/3 teaspoon almond extract

2 squares unsweetened chocolate melted

1 teaspoon gelatin

1/4 cup cold water

1/2 cup boiling water or milk

4 egg whites

1/2 cup sugar

1. Beat together the egg yolk, sugar, salt, and extracts.

2. Add the chocolate and beat until it is smooth.

3. Soften the gelatin in the 1/4 cup of cold water. Add boiling water and stir until the gelatin dissolves. Add this to the egg yolk-chocolate mixture.

4. Beat the egg whites stiff with 1/2 cup of sugar. Fold the egg whites into the chocolate mixture.

5. Let the mix cool and then pour it into a baked 9-inch pie shell and chill until it has firmed.

PUMPKIN PECAN PIE

Serving Size: 6 ounce

Total Servings: 6

3 eggs

1 cup canned pumpkin

2/3 cup corn syrup

1 cup sugar

2 tablespoons butter, melted

1 cup pecans

1/2 teaspoon cinnamon

1/4 teaspoon ginger

1/8 teaspoon cloves

1/2 teaspoon vanilla

Pumpkin Layer:

1. Stir together 1 egg, the canned pumpkin, 1/3 cup sugar, and the spices. Spread this in the bottom of a 9-inch unbaked pie shell.

Pecan Layer:

1. Stir together 2 eggs, the corn syrup, 2/3 cup sugar, 2 tablespoons butter, and vanilla.

2. Add the pecans.

3. Spoon this over the pumpkin mixture.

4. Bake at 350 degrees for 60 minutes or until set.

__Mother's Tip__

You can easily double this recipe. You can also take the pumpkins that you grew in your garden and use them to make the pie. Take two small pumpkins and cut the tops off and scoop out the seeds and strings. Put the top back on the pumpkins and pop them in a 250-degree oven until the pumpkin is soft—about 2 hours or so. After the pumpkin has cooled, scoop it out, and mash it up, use it in your favorite pumpkin recipes.

LEMON MERINGUE PIE

Serving Size: 6 ounce

Total Servings: 6

1 cup sugar

3 tablespoons cornstarch

1 1/2 cups boiling water

3 egg yolks

4 tablespoons lemon juice

2 tablespoons butter

1 baked 9-inch pie shell

4 egg whites

1/2 cup sugar

1. In a saucepan, mix the sugar, cornstarch, egg yolks, and lemon juice.

2. Add the water and cook until it has thickened. Do not let the mixture boil.

3. Add the butter and stir. Pour into a baked 9-inch pie shell and top with meringue.

4. To make the meringue, beat the 4 egg whites and 1/2 cup of sugar with an electric mixer on high speed until stiff peaks form.

5. Bake at 375 degrees until the meringue is a golden brown.

Mother's Tip

It is important to spread the meringue all the way to the edges of the pic shell to seal it. If you don't, it will shrink away from the edge of the pie after it has baked and expose the filling.

SOUTHERN PECAN PIE

Serving Size: 5 ounce

Total Servings: 6

1 cup sugar

1/2 cup white corn syrup

1/4 cup melted butter

3 eggs, well beaten

1 cup pecans

1 unbaked 8-inch pie shell

1. Combine the sugar, syrup, and melted butter.
2. Add the beaten eggs and pecans, and mix thoroughly.
3. Pour into the unbaked pie shell, and bake at 375 degrees for 40 to 45 minutes.

CINNAMON CAKE

Serving Size: 4 ounce

Total Servings: 10

1 cup shortening

2 cups sugar

4 unbeaten eggs

3 cups flour

3 teaspoons salt

1 cup milk

2 tablespoons cinnamon

2 tablespoons sugar

1. Combine the shortening and sugar.
2. Add the eggs, one at a time. Beat.
3. Add the dry ingredients, except for the cinnamon and sugar.
4. Add the milk.
5. Pour 1/2 the batter into a tube pan and sprinkle 1/2 the cinnamon and sugar.
6. Pour the rest of the batter on top of this and sprinkle the remaining sugar and cinnamon on top.
7. Bake at 350 degrees for 1 hour.

COCONUT SOUR CREAM POUND CAKE

Serving Size: 4 ounce

Total Servings: 9

3 sticks butter

2 cups sugar

6 eggs

3 cups flour

1/4 teaspoon baking soda

1/4 teaspoon salt

8 ounce sour cream

1 teaspoon vanilla

1 6-ounce package of flake coconut

1. Blend the butter and sugar.

2. Add the eggs, one at a time.

3. In a separate bowl, sift the flour, soda, and salt together.

4. Add this alternately with the sour cream.

5. Fold in the vanilla and coconut.

6. Bake in a 10-inch greased and floured pan or three small loaf pans at 350 degrees for 1 hour or longer, or until the cake is set in the middle.

Mother's Tip

If you use smaller pans, it will take less time (about 45 minutes). The cake is set in the middle if you stick a toothpick in the center and it comes out clean.

SEVEN-LAYER BARS

Serving Size: 3 ounce

Total Servings: 15

    1 cube butter, melted

    1 cup graham cracker crumbs

    1 cup coconut

    1 6-ounce package of butterscotch chips

    1 6-ounce package of chocolate chips

    1 can sweetened condensed milk

    1 cup nuts

1. Mix the butter and graham cracker crumbs, and press into a 9 x 13-inch pan.

2. Layer the coconut, then butterscotch chips, chocolate chips, milk, and nuts in that order on top of the crumbs.

3. Bake at 325–350 degrees for 30 minutes.

MY BEST BANANA BREAD RECIPE

Serving Size: 3 ounce

Total Servings: 16

1 cup sugar

1 cup butter

1/2 teaspoon salt

2 eggs

2 cups flour

1 teaspoon baking soda

1/2 cup walnuts

3 ripe bananas mashed

1. Mix together the sugar butter and salt in a medium sized bowl.

2. Beat the eggs into the butter mixture.

3. Mix the flour and baking soda into the mix and add the walnuts and bananas.

4. Spoon the batter into two bread pans and bake at 350 to 375 degrees for 1 hour.

CRINKLE COOKIES

Serving Size: 2 ounce

Total Servings: 36

  1 cup soft shortening

  1 cup brown sugar

  1 egg

  1/4 cup dark molasses

  1/4 cup milk

  2 3/4 cups sifted flour

  1 1/2 teaspoons soda

  1/4 teaspoon salt

  1 teaspoon cinnamon

  6 ounce of semi-sweet chocolate chips

  1/2 cup granulated sugar

1. Combine the shortening, brown sugar, egg, molasses, and milk. Mix thoroughly.

2. Sift the dry ingredients together in a separate bowl, then blend into the first mixture.

3. Fold in the chocolate pieces.

4. Chill for at least 1 hour, and then roll into walnut sized balls.

5. Dip these into the sugar and arrange sugar side up about 3 inches apart on a greased cookie sheet.

6. Bake at 375 degrees for about 10 minutes.

Mother's Tip

This is another of Grandma Blanche's recipes and is at least 40 years old.

CHEWY BROWNIES

Serving Size: 3 ounce

Total Servings: 15

4 beaten eggs

1 1/2 cups melted butter

3 heaping tablespoons cocoa

2 cups sugar

2 cups flour

1 cup nuts

1 cup powdered sugar

2 tablespoons hot coffee

1 1/2 tablespoons cocoa

1. Mix together the butter, sugar, and eggs.
2. Stir in the cocoa, flour, and nuts.
3. Pour it into a greased 9 x 13-inch pan.
4. Bake 15 to 20 minutes at 375 degrees.
5. Mix together the sugar, hot coffee, and cocoa to make the frosting.
6. Frost the brownies while they are hot.

What's For Dinner, Mom?

POTATO SOUP

Serving Size: 8 ounce

Total Servings: 6

> 6–8 potatoes, peeled and cut into bite sized pieces
>
> 1 leek, washed and cut into pieces
>
> 1 onion chopped
>
> 2 carrots, pared and sliced
>
> 4 chicken bouillon cubes
>
> 1 tablespoon parsley flakes
>
> 5 cups water
>
> 1/4 cup corn oil
>
> 1 13-ounce can of evaporated milk
>
> Scallions (optional)

1. Put all the ingredients except the evaporated milk and the scallions into a heavy kettle and bring to a boil. Lower the heat and simmer until the carrots are tender.
2. Stir in the evaporated milk and heat to boiling again.
3. Sprinkle the top with scallions and serve.

Mother's Tip

My Mom says that this can be put in a crock-pot on low for 10 hours, or high for 4 hours. You add the milk before the last hour.

GERMAN POTATO PANCAKES

Serving Size: 5 ounce

Total Servings: 6

4 large potatoes grated

2 egg yolks

1 teaspoon salt

1/2 scant cup flour

1/2 teaspoon baking powder or baking soda

3 tablespoons sour cream

2 egg whites beaten

1. Mix the potatoes, egg yolks, salt, flour, baking soda or powder, and the sour cream in a large bowl.

2. Fold in the beaten egg whites.

3. Use a large serving spoon to make individual pancakes.

4. Fry on a greased griddle until golden brown. Turn only once.

SKILLET CABBAGE

Serving Size: 6 ounce

Total Servings: 6

8 cups of cabbage chopped fine

2 tablespoons chopped onion

2 tablespoons butter

1/2 cup sour cream

Cayenne pepper and salt to taste

1. Cook and stir the cabbage and onion in a fry pan with melted butter until just tender.
2. Add seasonings and sour cream and heat, but don't boil.

Mother's Tip

This cabbage dish is especially good with pork roast or hamburger goulash.

PORK CHOP RICE CASSEROLE

Serving Size: 8 ounce

Total Servings: 4

4 or 5 pork chops

1$1/2$ cups uncooked rice

1 can beef consommé

1 can water

1. Wash or rinse pork chops to remove all particles of small bones.
2. Season with salt, pepper, and a little onion salt.
3. Brown in a skillet in a small amount of shortening.
4. Place the browned pork chops in a large casserole, and add the rice, beef consommé, and water.
5. Bake in oven at 325 for 1 hour. Check occasionally for moisture and add more water if necessary.

Mother's Tip

Soy sauce may be added by the individual at the table for added flavor.

SOUR CREAM PORK CHOPS

Serving Size: 8 to 10 ounce

Total Servings: 6

6 large pork chops

1 cup sour cream

1/2 package onion soup

1. Brown chops quickly over medium high heat.

2. Salt and pepper the pork chops.

3. Sprinkle onion soup over the chops and add sour cream. Cover and let simmer for 11/2 hours in electric skillet or Dutch oven.

TEMPTING LIVER

Serving Size: 4 ounce

Total Servings: 4-5

1 1/2 pound beef liver

3/4 cup flour

2 tablespoons butter

1 medium onion sliced thin

1 green bell pepper

1/2 cup chopped celery

1 12-ounce can diced tomatoes

2 tablespoons cornstarch

1. Cut 1 to 1 1/2 pound of liver in small pieces.
2. Flour both sides, and brown in a skillet in a little butter.
3. Add 1 sliced onion, 1 green pepper cut in thin strips, and 1/2 cup chopped celery. Pour the tomatoes over all of it.
4. Cover the skillet with a lid and let simmer for 20 to 30 minutes.
5. Mix 2 tablespoons of cornstarch in a bit of water and pour into liver to thicken.

Mother's Tip

This is delicious server over either white or brown rice.

LAMB CHOPS WITH CORNBREAD STUFFING

Serving Size: 8-10 ounce

Total Servings: 4

Non-stick spray coating

4 American lamb shoulder chops 3/4 to 1 inch thick (about 134 pound)

11/3 cup water

2 tablespoons butter

1 package or 6 ounce cornbread stuffing

1 11-ounce can corn with red and green peppers

1. Spray a 10-inch skillet with the non-stick spray. Cook the chops over medium high heat for 4 to 5 minutes, turning once, until nicely browned.

2. Remove the chops from the pan; reduce the heat to low.

3. Add water, butter, and vegetable seasoning from the cornbread packet; mix well. Stir in undrained corn and crumbs from the mix until well blended.

4. Place the lamb chops on top of the stuffing.

5. Cover and cook over low heat for 10 to 12 minutes or until chops are well done.

YUM YUMS

Serving Size: 4 Ounce

Total Servings: 6

1 pound lean hamburger

2/3 cup catsup or tomato juice

1 teaspoon prepared mustard

1 tablespoon brown sugar

1 tablespoon vinegar

1 tablespoon flour

Salt and pepper

1. Lightly brown the hamburger and onion.

2. Drain off the grease. Return to the stove, and add the catsup, prepared mustard, brown sugar, vinegar, flour, and salt and pepper.

3. Simmer for 20 minutes, and serve over hot buns.

MOM'S SALMON PATTIES

Serving Size: 6 ounce

Total Servings: 8

1 14 3/4 -ounce pink salmon, including the liquid and bones

1 10 3/4 -ounce cream of celery soup, reserve 1/4 cup for the sauce

11/2 cups crushed herb seasoned stuffing mix

1/3 cup finely chopped onion

1 large egg

3 tablespoons milk

1/2 teaspoon dried dill weed

1. Mix the salmon, soup, stuffing mix, onion, and egg in a medium sized bowl and then form into eight patties.

2. Fry the patties in a lightly greased non-stick skillet on medium heat for about 2 to 3 minutes on each side until lightly browned.

3. To make the dill sauce, mix the 1/4 cup reserved cream of celery soup, milk, and dry dill weed in a small bowl and serve with the patties.

Mother's Tip

You can also put the salmon in a lightly greased 1/2-quart loaf pan, and bake in a 350 degree oven for 40 minutes or until firm to the touch.

HOT MACARONI AND TOMATO

Serving Size: 7 ounce

Total Servings: 5

16-ounce package small elbow macaroni

1 large can stewed tomatoes

1 tablespoon butter

2 tablespoons butter

1. Cook the macaroni according to the package direction and drain the water off.

2. Add the rest of the ingredients to the macaroni and simmer for about 30 minutes.

Mother's Tip

I don't know what it is about this recipe, but it is so delicious. My mom made it often when I was a child. She says it was a good filler when she was trying to fill the tummies of three active children.

SPARERIBS AND SAUERKRAUT

Serving Size: 10 Ounce

Total Servings: 6

4 pound pork spareribs with bone in

1 24-ounce can sauerkraut

1 bay leaf

Salt and pepper

1. Place the spareribs in a large pot and cover with water. Bring to a boil, and then lower the heat and simmer until the meat is tender. You will have to skim the water 2 or 3 times during cooking.

2. Add the bay leaf and salt and pepper when the ribs are simmering.

3. When the ribs are tender, take out the bay leaf and add the sauerkraut.

Mother's Tip

Mother always served mounds of mashed potatoes with this meal and nothing else. It is very filling. This is probably the meal we all liked the best.

HELEN'S POT ROAST

Serving Size: 12 ounce

Total Servings: 6

4 pound chuck or rump roast

2 bay leaves

6 potatoes, halved and then quartered

1/2 large onion, cut in quarters

3 large carrots, cleaned, pared, sliced in half and then in quarters

1/2 head cabbage, quartered

1. Place meat in a large roaster. Salt and pepper the meat and fill the roaster 1/2 full with water. Add the bay leaves.

2. Put the roast in the oven at 375 degrees for 11/2 to 2 hours until the meat is tender. Add more water if necessary.

3. Add cut up potatoes, carrots, onion, and cabbage, and cook for 1 more hour.

Mother's Tip

My brothers and I liked to smash up the carrots and potatoes and pour the juice from the roast over them. If we ran out of potatoes, we used white bread torn into pieces with the broth poured over it. There was always a stack of white bread on a plate at all our meals. If you were still hungry, you just grabbed some bread and buttered it and filled up.

SPECIAL HAMBURGERS

Serving Size: 7 ounce

Total Servings: 8

2 pound lean hamburger

1/2 small onion chopped fine

8 Saltine crackers

1 large egg

1. Crush Saltines in your hand.

2. Beat the egg in a bowl. Add all the saltines and onion together with the egg.

3. Mix well.

4. Pat out nice sized patties, and fry to a medium well temperature.

MILD CHILI

Serving Size: 6 ounce

Total Servings: 8

1 pound hamburger browned and drained of fat

1 large can kidney beans

1 large can pinto beans

1 small can tomato paste

1 small onion chopped

Chili powder to taste

1. Brown the hamburger and onion together, and drain off the grease.
2. Mix the hamburger, kidney and pinto beans, tomato paste, onion, and chili powder in a big pot.
3. Cover the beans and hamburger with water. Simmer for about 1 hour so that all the flavors can meld together.
4. Serve with chunks of sharp cheddar cheese and saltine crackers.

STUFFED CABBAGE ROLLS

Serving Size: 7ounce

Total Servings: 6

1 pound ground beef

1/2 pound ground pork

3 cups cooked rice

1 teaspoon sugar

1 onion chopped

1 teaspoon salt

1/4 teaspoon pepper

1 head cabbage

1 tablespoon butter

1 cup water

1 101/2-ounce can cream of tomato soup

1. Combine the beef, pork, rice, sugar, onion, salt, and pepper.
2. Wilt the cabbage leaves by placing in boiling water for a few minutes.
3. Place about ½ of the mixture in each cabbage leaf and roll up securely.
4. Place the rolls in a 13 x 9-inch baking pan. Dot each roll with butter.
5. Combine the water and soup, and pour over the rolls. Bake at 350 for 1 hour or until the rolls are well done.

POTATO PANCAKES

Serving Size: 8 ounce

Total Servings: 6

2–3 cups leftover mashed potatoes

1 cup flour

2 eggs

1 teaspoon baking powder

Pinch of sugar

1 cup milk, cream, or half and half

1. Mix all the ingredients together, and stir until it is smooth and looks like pancake batter.

2. Cook on a griddle just like pancakes, browning on each side. Serve with bacon and fried eggs.

KATOFEL KLASE (POTATOES AND DUMPLINGS)

Serving Size: 8 ounce

Total Servings: 5

> 2 or 3 medium potatoes
>
> 1 tablespoon salt
>
> 3 eggs
>
> 2 quarts water
>
> 1/2 cup butter

Klase Dough

Serving Size: 8 ounces

Total Servings: 6

> 2-quarts boiling water
>
> 1 cup flour
>
> 1 egg
>
> 1/2 teaspoon baking powder
>
> 1/2 teaspoon salt
>
> 1/4 cup milk or more for soft dough
>
> 4 large eggs

1. Bring the 2 quarts of water to boiling. Add the salt and potatoes. Boil the potatoes until they are almost done. Leave the potatoes in the boiling water.

2. Mix the flour, baking powder, salt, milk, and egg together and spoon the dough, a tablespoon at a time, into the boiling water.

3. Dip the spoon in the hot water each time so the dough doesn't stick to the spoon.

4. Cook the dumplings with the lid on the pot for about 10 minutes and then drain the water off the potatoes and klase or dumplings.

5. Fry the potatoes and dumplings in butter in a large fry pan until lightly browned.

6. Lightly beat the eggs and mix into the potatoes and klase, covering for just a few minutes.

Mother's Tip

Klase can be topped with buttered bread crumbs, sour cream, or leftover sauerkraut.

BAKED OMELET

Serving Size: 6 ounce

Total Servings: 10

  1 dozen eggs, beaten

  12 slices white bread, diced

  2 cups milk

  8 ounce diced ham

  1$1/2$ pound grated cheese

  Salt and pepper

  1. Mix all the ingredients, and bake 1 hour in a buttered 9 x 13-inch pan at 350 degrees.

  2. Remove from the oven and let set for about 10 minutes.

PLAIN SWISS STEAK

Serving Size: 10 ounce

Total Servings: 4

1 pound round shoulder or chuck steak cut 1 inch thick

1 teaspoon salt

1 medium onion

1/3 cup cooking oil

1 cup tomato juice

1 cup flour

1. Rub the meat with the salt.

2. Sprinkle the flour over the steak and pound all the flour possible into the steak using a meat mallet. Brown the floured and tenderized meat in the hot oil.

3. Add the tomato juice to cover the steak.

4. Slice the onion over the steak, and simmer until the meat is tender.

BEEF STROGANOFF

Serving Size: 10 ounce

Total Servings: 5

11/2 to 2 pound round steak

3/4 cup water

3 tablespoons flour

1 can French onion soup

1 can or 1 cup fresh mushrooms (any kind)

1. Cut the steak into 1 x 2-inch pieces, roll in flour, and brown in the oil.

2. Add the onion soup and mushrooms (including the mushroom juice if canned).

3. Simmer until the meat is tender, 45 minutes to 1 hour.

4. Remove from the heat and add the sour cream.

5. Serve over cooked noodles or rice.

AMERICAN CHOP SUEY

Serving Size: 10 ounce

Total Servings: 6

1 3/4 pound lean ground beef

1 medium chopped onion

3 cans Campbell's tomato soup undiluted

Approximately 3/4 of a 12-ounce package of elbow macaroni

Grated parmesan cheese

1. In a large frying pan, sauté the chopped onion until tender. Add the hamburger and cook until it is no longer red.

2. Cook the macaroni until it is tender. Add the drained macaroni to the burger and onions.

3. Now add the tomato soup and mix thoroughly.

4. Sprinkle with parmesan and mix. Sprinkle more parmesan on top and serve.

Mother's Tip

This recipe came from my husband David's mother Eleanor. All the men in her family adored this dish and always asked for it when they came to visit her. She made this recipe up herself and served it long ago when David was a child. I think the secret is the undiluted soup. She gave the name American Chop Suey to this recipe.

SWEET PORK CHOPS

Serving Size: 10 ounce

Total Servings: 6

6–8 pork chops, any kind

Salt

Graham cracker crumbs

1. Salt the pork chops and dredge in graham cracker crumbs.

2. Place in a large baking pan, and spread the remaining crumbs on the top of the chops.

3. Bake at 350 degrees for 30 to 40 minutes, depending on the thickness of the pork chops.

Mother's Tip

Serve the pork chops with cubed boiled new red potatoes with the skins left on. Add butter, milk, salt, and pepper. Do not mash them. This is a recipe that was given to me eons ago by a good friend. I have used it countless times. It is simple and quick, especially if you have last minute company coming.

SWEET AND SOUR LAMB CHOPS

Serving Size: 10 ounce

Total Servings: 4

4 shoulder lamb chops about 1 -inch thick

1/4 cup brown sugar

1/4 cup vinegar

1/2 teaspoon ground ginger

4 orange slices

4 lemon wedges

1 tablespoon cornstarch

1. In a large skillet, brown the lamb chops on both sides over a low heat.

2. Combine the brown sugar, vinegar, ginger, 1 teaspoon salt, and a dash of pepper; pour this over the meat and top each chop with an orange slice and a lemon wedge.

3. Cover; cook over low heat for about 30 minutes until the meat is tender.

4. Remove the lamb from the skillet and move to a warm platter.

5. Pour the pan juices into a measuring cup, skim off the fat, and then add water to make 1 cup of juice. Return this liquid to the skillet.

6. Blend the cornstarch and 1 tablespoon of cold water; stir into the liquid. Cook and stir this until the mixture is boiling.

7. Serve the lamb chops with brown rice and pour the sauce over all.

OLD-TIME BEEF STEW

Serving Size: 8 ounce

Total Servings: 8

2 pound beef chuck cut into 1 1/2-inch cubes or 2 pound stew meat

1 teaspoon Worcestershire sauce

1 medium onion chopped coarse

1 or 2 bay leaves

1 tablespoon salt

1 teaspoon sugar

1/4 teaspoon pepper

Dash ground allspice or cloves

6 carrots pared and quartered

4 potatoes pared and quartered

1 package frozen peas or corn or both

1 cup flour

1. Dredge the stew meat in the flour, and then in a Dutch oven over medium heat, thoroughly brown the meat in 2 tablespoons shortening, turning often.

2. Add 2 cups of hot water and add the Worcestershire, onion, bay leaves, salt, sugar, pepper, and allspice or cloves.

3. Cover. Simmer for 1 1/2 hours, stirring occasionally to keep everything from sticking.

4. Remove the bay leaves, and add the vegetables.

5. Cover and cook for 35 to 40 minutes, or until the vegetables are tender.

6. Skim any fat from the liquid part of the stew.

7. Take out 1 3/4 cup broth. Combine 1/4 cup water and 2 tablespoon of flour and stir until smooth. Slowly stir this into the hot broth you removed from the stew. Return all of this to the stew, cook, and stir until bubbly. Cook and stir for 3 minutes more.

Mothers Tips

This is a thick stew; chunks of sharp cheddar cheese and slices of homemade bread are a tasty addition. The stew will keep for a week in the refrigerator, or it can be put in plastic containers and frozen.

GERMAN FLANZES

Serving Size: 2 ounce

Total Servings: 4

2 cups flour

5 eggs

1 teaspoon salt

1 cup cream or half and half

1/2 stick butter melted

1. Mix the flour, eggs, and salt, and thin with milk until you have a running dough like a pancake batter.

2. Pour very thin, about three -inches across, and bake on a pancake griddle.

3. Turn them over with a pancake turner and lightly brown the other side.

4. Remove from the heat and fold twice.

5. Stir together the cream and melted butter.

6. Dip each flanze in the bowl of cream and melted butter.

7. Put in layers into a dish; place the dish into a shallow pan of water that has been placed in a 350-degree oven and steam the flanzes for 1 hour.

8. Serve with maple syrup.

VEGETABLE SOUP (KRAUT SUPPE)

Serving Size: 8 ounce

Total Servings: 6

3 carrots

3 potatoes

1/4 cup onion

3 cups finely shredded cabbage

1/2 cup celery

2 1/2 pound beef or soup bone

1 bay leaf

Salt and pepper to taste

1 medium can tomatoes

1. Wash the carrots, potatoes, and cabbage. Peel the potatoes and carrots.
2. Chop all the vegetables very fine.
3. Boil the beef or soup bone and bay leaves in 2 quarts of water in a large, heavy pot until the meat is tender.
4. Add all the vegetables. When they are nearly done, about one hour, add the tomatoes and simmer about 20 more minutes until all is done.
5. Discard the soup bone and bay leaf.

Mother's Tip

This is delicious served with German light rye bread. You can double this recipe and have soup to freeze or serve later in the week. The more you cook it, the better it gets.

GERMAN SOUP (FOR THE SICK)

Serving Size: 6 ounce

Total Servings: 1

3 ounce butter

3 to 4 tablespoons flour

2/3 cup water or milk

2 to 3 slices of white toast

1. Put 3 ounce of butter into a pan and heat it until brown.

2. Stir 3 or 4 tablespoons of flour into the butter and brown.

3. Add enough cold water to make a soup consistency.

4. Toast 2 to 3 slices of bread. Tear the pieces of bread up, put into the milk, and heat through. Add as much salt and pepper as you like.

5. Serve in a big coffee mug with a soup spoon.

Mother's Tip

My father always asked for this soup when he was sick. Even when he was in the hospital, we would have to ask them to make this soup. He called it "Chai." It was very tasty and settled the stomach immediately

SWEET STUFFING FOR CHICKEN OR TURKEY

Serving Size: 8 ounce

Total Servings: 4

Giblets and liver from a chicken or turkey

1 cup raisins

1 large peeled apple

2 cups plain bread crumbs

1/2 cup sugar

2 eggs

1 teaspoon cinnamon

1/2 teaspoon salt

1 cup milk or 1 cup broth that the giblets have been cooked

1 12-pound turkey or 1 5-pound chicken

1. Take and cook the giblets and liver from a chicken or turkey. Put in a medium saucepan, cover with water, bring to a boil, and then simmer the giblets and liver for 30 minutes.

2. Grind together 1 cup raisins, 1 large peeled apple, and the giblets. Use a food processor or blender.

3. Mix the ground up raisins, apple, and giblets with 2 cups of bread crumbs, 1/2 cup of sugar, 2 eggs, salt, 1 teaspoon of cinnamon, and 1 cup of milk or broth in which the giblets have been cooked.

4. Mix thoroughly and spoon into the chicken or turkey cavity. The extra dressing can be put into a greased casserole dish and baked in the oven along with the chicken or turkey. Bake the chicken and dressing at 375 degrees for 1 hour. The turkey should be baked at

350 degrees and according to the poundage from 2 to 4 hours.

5. This makes enough for a 5- or 6-pound chicken or 1 12-pound turkey.

Mother's Tip

My father is the only one in our family who liked this dish. It has an apple cinnamon flavor. Crumbled cornbread may be substituted for the plain breadcrumbs.

MEAT LOAF

Serving Size: 8 ounce

Total Servings: 6

2 pound hamburger

1/2 cup finely chopped onion

1/4 teaspoon minced garlic

2 eggs

1/2 cup ketchup

1/2 teaspoon salt

1/2 teaspoon pepper

20 Saltine crackers crushed fine

1/2 to 1 cup milk

4 bacon strips

1. Put the 2 pound of hamburger in a big bowl and break the eggs over it.
2. Mix in the chopped onion, minced garlic, ketchup, salt, pepper, and the Saltines crushed fine.
3. Pour the milk over the hamburger mixture to make it very moist.
4. Put the meat loaf in a bread pan and lay bacon strips on the top. Bake it in the oven at 350 to 375 degrees for 45 minutes to an hour.

Mother's Tip

Serve with mashed potatoes (skins on) and French cut green beans. This is a flexible recipe, so you can add more saltines, less milk, or more garlic to suit your own taste.

APPLE PORK CHOPS

Serving Size: 12 ounce

Total Servings: 6

2 unpeeled apples, thinly sliced

1 cup brown sugar

1 tablespoon cinnamon

1/2 cup butter

6 center cut pork chops

1. Thinly slice 2 unpeeled apples into a greased 13 x 9-inch pan.

2. Sprinkle 1 cup of brown sugar over the apples. Sprinkle 1 tablespoon of cinnamon over apples and brown sugar. Dot with pats of butter.

3. Brown 6 pork chops in a separate fry pan, drain, and place on top of the apples.

4. Cover the chops and bake at 325 degrees to 350 degrees for 1 hour.

Mother's Tip

Serve with brown rice and steamed carrots. Spoon the apples over the pork chops before serving.

THANKSGIVING STUFFING FOR TURKEY

Serving Size: 8 ounce

Total Servings: 12

1 loaf white bread

1 loaf wheat bread

Giblets and liver from turkey

1 cup butter

1 medium white onion

2 tablespoons sage

1 teaspoon rosemary

1 teaspoon thyme

1/2 teaspoon basil

1/2 teaspoon tarragon

6 to 8 cups chicken broth or water from cooking the giblets

1 tablespoon salt

1 14-pound turkey

1. About 1 month ahead of time take a loaf of white bread and a loaf of wheat bread and tear it into little pieces and put it into a big dishpan; cover it with a tea towel and let it dry. Stir it once a week so that all the bread is dried.

2. On Thanksgiving morning, boil the turkey giblets in salted water, drain, cool, and rough chop them.

3. Dice one medium onion, and then melt 1 cup of butter.

4. Place the bread in a large mixing bowl, and sprinkle the herbs over the bread.

5. Put the onion in with the bread crumbs, and pour the melted butter over the top.

6. Mix all the ingredients, then pour warm chicken broth over the mixture, and stir. Use enough broth for the stuffing to be super moist.

7. Clean the inside of the turkey with cold water and lightly salt it inside and out. Preheat the oven to 375 degrees.

8. Stuff the turkey and put the rest of the stuffing in a large roasting pan and put into the oven with the turkey 45 minutes to 1 hour before the turkey is done.

9. Bake the 14-pound turkey for 2 1/2 hours. Baste it every 30 minutes.

Mother's Tip

The turkey does not have to be stuffed. It can all be cooked in a big roasting pan. If you don't have the stuffing in the turkey, put quartered apples and onion in the turkey cavity to add flavor to the turkey meat. This stuffing is very good with turkey gravy poured over it.

SCALLOPED POTATOES AND HAM

Serving Size: 8 ounce

Total Servings: 6

6 medium potatoes, sliced

1 cup diced ham

Salt and pepper

1 cup milk or half and half

1 cup buttered breadcrumbs

1 tablespoon butter

1. Parboil the sliced potatoes for 10 minutes. The potatoes will only by partially cooked.

2. Layer the potatoes in a buttered 9 x 13-inch glass casserole dish, and sprinkle with salt and pepper and breadcrumbs.

3. Add the ham, and dot with butter.

4. Repeat these layers until the dish is full.

5. Pour the milk over the potatoes, and bake at 350 degrees for about 1 hour.

BAKED EGGPLANT

Serving Size: 6 ounce

Total Servings: 4

1 medium eggplant

1/4 cup butter

1/2 cup crushed Saltine crackers

1 teaspoon chopped onion

2 eggs

Salt and pepper

1. Preheat the oven to 400 degrees.
2. Pare the eggplant and cut into 1/4 -inch slices.
3. Cook in salt water until tender.
4. Drain the water off and add butter, Saltines, onion, and eggs.
5. Season with salt and pepper, and bake in a 9 x 9-inch glass casserole dish in a 400 degree oven until brown.

POTATOES AND NOODLES

Serving Size: 8 ounce

Total Servings: 4

1 large diced potato

2 quarts water

Salt and pepper

11/4 cups uncooked noodles

1/4 cup butter

2/3 cup cubed white bread

1. Boil 1 large diced potato in 2 quarts of water seasoned with salt and pepper.

2. When the potato is done, add 11/4 cups of uncooked noodles to the potato; add more water if needed to cover the noodles and potatoes. Cook about 12 minutes and drain well.

3. In a skillet, melt 1/4 cup of butter and sauté 2/3 cup of cubed bread. Sauté until the bread is golden brown and then add the potato noodle mixture.

4. Cook about 8 minutes, stirring 4 or 5 times.

Mother's Tip

This is great served with fried chicken or sliced ham.

SALAD OR SALAT

WILTED LETTUCE OR SALAT SPECK

Serving Size: 10 ounce

Total Servings: 6

1 large bowl of dark leaf lettuce that has been thoroughly washed

1 large tomato

1/4 cup chopped onion

1/4 pound bacon fried

11/4 cup of half and half

1 to 2 tablespoons vinegar

Salt and pepper to taste

1. Fry the bacon. Set aside the fry pan and 1/4 cup bacon grease.

2. In a large bowl, tear the lettuce into bite size pieces. Mix the chopped tomato, onion, and bacon into the lettuce.

3. Heat the bacon grease until it is hot.

4. Mix the vinegar into the half and half and slowly whisk this into the bacon grease. Stir until the mixture is heated through.

5. Pour over the lettuce, stir, and serve immediately.

FRESH CUCUMBER SALAD
GOMEN SALUTE

Serving Size: 8 ounce

Total Servings: 8

8 medium cucumbers

4 hard boiled eggs

1/8 cup chopped onion

1/2 pint buttermilk

Salt and pepper

1. Slice the cucumbers into a large bowl, medium thickness.
2. Chop the eggs, but not too fine.
3. Chop the onion and mix together with the eggs and cucumbers. Sprinkle quite a bit of salt and pepper over it all.
4. Pour the buttermilk over the mixture and mix well. Let set for 1 hour for the flavors to meld.

Mother's Tip

This recipe is good with any kind of fried sausage and crusty bread.

CABBAGE SALAD
KRAUT SALUTE

Serving Size: 6 ounce

Total Servings: 4

3 cups finely chopped cabbage

1/2 fine cut apple

1/2 cup Miracle Whip

4 tablespoons sugar

1/4 cup green pepper, cut fine

1/4 cup chopped onion

1 tablespoon vinegar

1. Put cabbage, pepper, onion, and apple into a medium bowl.

2. Mix together Miracle Whip, vinegar, and sugar and pour over the cabbage. Mix well.

COTTAGE CHEESE SALAD

Serving Size: 6 ounce

Total Servings: 4

1 carton of medium curd creamy cottage cheese

1 medium cucumber

1 small tomato

1/8 cup onion

Salt and pepper

1. Chop the cucumber, tomato, and onion fairly fine, and mix it into the cottage cheese.

2. Add salt and pepper to taste.

Mother's Tip

I don't know how or when Mom started making this salad, but I've never found it anywhere else. It's better if the cucumber and tomato are fresh out of the garden. Radishes and onions instead or tomatoes and cucumbers are good also.

COLESLAW

1-quart cabbage

4 stalks celery

2 medium carrots

1/4 cup vinegar

1/4 cup sugar

1/2 cup mayonnaise

Salt and pepper

1. Shred enough cabbage to make 1 quart. Chop it very fine.

2. Grate 4 stalks of celery and 2 carrots. Soak in salted water in the refrigerator for 1 hour. Press out all of the water.

3. Mix ¼ cup vinegar and 1/4 cup of sugar, and stir in 1/2 cup of mayonnaise. Add to the cabbage.

4. Add salt to taste and let stand in the fridge for awhile to blend the flavors.

SEVEN LAYER SALAD

Serving Size: 8 ounce

Total Servings: 12

  6 cups chopped lettuce

  Salt and pepper

  6 hard boiled eggs, sliced

  2 cups frozen peas, thawed

  16 ounce bacon, fried crisp and crumbled

  2 cups shredded mild cheddar cheese

  1 cup mayonnaise

  1 to 2 tablespoons sugar

  1/4 cup sliced green onion with tops

  Paprika

1. Place 3 cups of the lettuce in the bottom of a 9 x 13-inch glass Pyrex pan; sprinkle with salt and pepper.

2. Layer the egg slices over the lettuce and sprinkle with more salt and pepper.

3. Continue to layer the vegetables in this order: peas, remaining lettuce, crumbled bacon, and shredded cheese.

4. Combine the mayonnaise and sugar; spread over the top of the salad to the edge of the bowl to cover the entire salad.

5. Cover and chill overnight or 24 hours.

6. Garnish with green onion and a little paprika. Sprinkle a little more shredded cheddar on top for color before serving.

POTATO SALAD

Serving Size: 6 ounce

Total Servings: 7

4 cups diced, cooked potatoes

1 teaspoon salt

1/4 teaspoon pepper

1 medium onion, diced

1/2 cup chopped sweet pickles

4 hard-boiled eggs

1/4 cup pickle juice or 2 tablespoons vinegar

1 tablespoon mustard

1 cup mayonnaise

1. Combine potatoes, salt, pepper, onion, pickles, and diced eggs.

2. Blend the pickle juice and mustard into the mayonnaise and add to the potato mixture.

3. Mix the ingredients well, cover, and refrigerate overnight.

Mother's Tip

You can easily double or triple this recipe for larger groups. You can also substitute pasta for the potatoes. My family likes the pasta better. I sometimes use dill pickle instead of sweet pickle, and if the dressing is a bit too tart, I will add a wee bit of sugar.

CAULIFLOWER CHEESE SALAD

Serving Size: 8 ounce

Total Servings: 10

1 cup mayonnaise

1/4 cup sugar

1 large head cauliflower, chopped

1 large green pepper, chopped

1 pound bacon, cooked, drained, and chopped

1 cup shredded Colby cheese

1. In a small bowl, combine the mayonnaise and sugar and set aside.
2. In a large bowl, combine cauliflower, green pepper, onion, bacon, and cheese.
3. Pour the mayonnaise dressing over the vegetables.
4. Mix and refrigerate.

BREAD OR BROT

STONE GROUND BREAD FROM BLANCH INNES

Serving Size: 4 ounce

Total Servings: 16 slices

2 cups milk

1/2 cup honey

1/2 cup sugar

1 tablespoon salt

1/4 cup shortening

2 cakes yeast dissolved in 1/2 cup water

3 cups sifted stone ground wheat flour

1 cup sifted whole-wheat flour

2 cups sifted white flour

1. Scald the milk in a small heavy saucepan.
2. Add the honey, sugar, salt and shortening to the scalded milk.
3. When this mixture has cooled, add the yeast.
4. Pour the ingredients into a large mixing bowl and add the flours, one cup at a time.
5. Mix and knead for five minutes or until the dough has a satiny appearance.
6. Cover the dough and let rise for 45 minutes to one hour.

7. Divide the dough into 2 equal parts and place into 2 greased and floured bread pans.

8. Let rise for 45 minutes.

9. Place in a 350 degree oven and bake for one hour.

10. Remove the bread from the oven and remove from the bread pans at once

11. Cool the 2 loaves on a wire rack

RYE BREAD

Serving Size: 6 ounce

Total Servings: 16 slices

   4 cups potato water

   1 1/2 cups rye flour

   1 cup white flour

   1/2 cup whole-wheat flour

   1/4 cup sugar

   1/4 cup Mazola Oil

   1 teaspoon salt

   3 cups white flour

1. Mix the potato water, rye flour, white flour, whole-wheat flour, and sugar in a large mixing bowl. Cover with a clean towel, and place in a warm area.

2. Let the mix raise once and beat it down. Let it rise again, and add enough of the 3 cups of flour to make a stiff dough. You do not have to use all of the flour.

3. Mix 1/4 cup Mazola oil and 1 teaspoon salt into the dough.

4. Let it raise and knead down.

5. Put the dough in two bread pans and bake about 50 minutes at 350 degrees.

Mother's Tip

This is my father's sister's recipe—Aunt Mary Schwartz. Be sure you grease the bread pans for all homemade bread recipes. The loaves of bread will just fall out of the pan and never stick to the sides if you remember to do this

WHITE BREAD

Serving Size: 6 ounce

Total Servings: 16 slices

1 1/4 cups lukewarm water

1 cake yeast or 1 package

1 cup milk scalded

2 tablespoons sugar

2 teaspoons salt

2 tablespoons shortening

6 1/2 to 7 cups sifted white flour

1. Dissolve the yeast and 1 teaspoon of sugar in 1/4 cup lukewarm water. Let this stand 10 minutes.
2. Scald the milk.
3. Add sugar, salt, water, and shortening to the milk. Cool to lukewarm.
4. Gradually add the yeast mixture and flour. Beat thoroughly after each addition.
5. Turn the dough onto a floured board and knead for about 10 minutes.
6. Shape the dough into a ball and place in a greased bowl. Brush the top lightly with melted shortening.
7. Melt the shortening in a small saucepan on low heat on top of the stove.
8. Cover the dough, and let it rise until it has doubled.
9. Divide the dough in two and place in two greased bread pans.

10. Cover and let rise until it has doubled.

11. Bake at 375 degrees for about 50 minutes.

BANANA NUT BREAD

Serving Size: 4 ounce

Total Servings: 8 thick slices

1 cup sugar

1 cup butter

1/2 teaspoon salt

2 eggs

2 cups flour

1 teaspoon soda

1/2 cup walnuts (optional)

3 ripe bananas mashed

1. Cream sugar, butter, and salt ingredients. Add the eggs, flour, soda, walnuts, and bananas.

2. Mix all of the ingredients well, put into a loaf pan, and bake for 1 hour at 375 degrees.

Mother's Tip

Use the tiny little throw away aluminum loaf pans and make smaller servings and freeze the rest. If you use the smaller pans, bake the bread for 45 minutes. You can double and triple this recipe.

ORANGE RYE BREAD

Serving Size: 6 ounce

Total Servings: 16 slices

3 3/4 cups warm water (105–115 degrees)

2 packages dry yeast

1/2 cup brown sugar, firmly packed

3 tablespoons butter

5 1/2 to 6 1/2 cups white flour, unsifted

4 teaspoons salt

3 tablespoons grated orange peel

1/3 cup dark molasses

3 3/4 cups rye flour, unsifted

1. Measure the warm water into a large warm bowl.
2. Sprinkle in the yeast; stir until the yeast is dissolved.
3. Stir in the sugar, salt, butter, orange peel, molasses, and rye flour.
4. Beat until this is thoroughly blended.
5. Stir in enough white flour to make a stiff dough.
6. Turn onto a lightly floured board and knead until it is smooth and elastic, about 10–12 minutes.
7. Place in a greased bowl, turning it over once to grease the top.
8. Cover and let rise in a warm place, free from draft, until it has doubled in bulk, about 1 hour.
9. Punch the dough down and divide in half.

10. Roll each half to a 14 x 9-inch rectangle.

11. Shape into loaves.

12. Place into two greased 9 x 5 x 3-inch loaf pans.

13. Cover and let rise in a warm place, free from draft, until it has doubled in bulk, about 1 hour and 10 minutes.

14. Bake in a preheated oven on the lowest rack at 375 degrees for 40 minutes.

15. Remove from the pans and cool on wire racks.

16. While the bread is hot, brush the tops with melted butter.

BROWN SODA BREAD

Serving Size: 6 ounce

Total Servings: 10 wedges

1 pound white flour

1 pound whole wheat flour

2 level teaspoons sugar

2 level teaspoons of bread soda

2 level teaspoons salt

1. Mix all of the ingredients and then make a well in the center. Gradually add 1 pint of thick sour milk or buttermilk.

2. Put in the oven at 400 degrees for 10 minutes, and then reduce the heat to 350 degrees for about 30 minutes more.

3. Wrap the bread in a damp tea towel to keep it moist after it comes out of the oven.

PFEFFERNIESS

Serving Size: 4 ounce

Total Servings: 20 rolls

    1 cup scalded milk

    1/4 cup shortening

    1 cake yeast or 1 package

    1/4 cup sugar

    1 teaspoon salt

    1/2 cup warm water

    1/2 cup dark molasses

    4 cups flour or enough for a soft dough

    Pinch of pepper

    1 well beaten egg

    1/2 teaspoon anise oil

1. Soak the yeast in warm water until soft, then add remaining ingredients, and mix well.

2. Let rise until double. Knead down and let rise again.

3. Knead down again and shape into small rolls. Place the shaped dough into a 9 x 13-inch pan.

4. Let rise again until the rolls have doubled and then bake at 375 degrees for 40 minutes.

BLINA (GERMAN PANCAKES)

Serving Size: 6 ounce:

Total Servings: 6

2 cups flour

1 cup warm water

1 package yeast

1 egg

Pinch of salt

1/4 teaspoon baking powder

About 1/2 cup milk

1. Mix flour, warm water, and yeast the evening before. Refrigerate.

2. The following morning, mix the egg, salt, and baking power into the sponge you made the night before.

3. Thin the batter with a little warm milk, about 1/4 cup.

4. Pour 1/2 cup of the batter into a hot greased skillet. Tip the skillet slowly from side to side to cover the entire bottom.

5. Use moderate heat and fry until the cake appears dry. Turn the cake for a brief time until the edges are brown.

6. Serve with syrup or sugar.

CINNAMON ROLLS

Serving Size: 6 ounce

Total Servings: 15

1 cup milk

1 cake yeast

1/4 cup sugar

3 cups flour

1 cup brown sugar

2 teaspoons cinnamon

1 teaspoon salt

2 eggs, beaten

1/4 cup salad oil

4 tablespoons butter

1/4 cup water

1. Scald the milk and when it is lukewarm, add the yeast, sugar, and 11/2 cups of flour. Mix it together.

2. When it is bubbly, add the salt, eggs, oil, and remaining flour.

3. Knead the dough well for about 5 minutes, place in a large greased mixing bowl, cover with a clean towel, and let it rise until doubled.

4. Roll out the dough 1/4 inch thick and 11 inches wide and 15 inches long.

5. Spread 3 tablespoons of butter over the dough, and then sprinkle with cinnamon and 1/2 cup of the brown sugar.

6. Roll the dough up like a jellyroll and slice 1 inch thick.

7. Place in a greased 11 x 15-inch pan. Let the rolls rise again.

8. Before baking, mix the remaining 1/2 cup of brown sugar, the remaining 1 tablespoon of butter, and 1/4 cup of water and pour over the rolls.

9. Bake at 350 degrees for 35 minutes. This yields 12 to 15 rolls. You can add pecans to this recipe if you wish.

Black and White Memories

John and Susanna Nab

My father Harold and his brother, Uncle Ted

Harold and Ted on Shorty

Beautiful Mom Helen at 16

Courting

The wedding photo of Harold and Helen in 1940

Harold and Helen, married 1 year

My brother Ron

My brother Tim

Baby Rebecca

Harold and Helen going to church

Rebecca and Santa

Helen and her sisters, Esther, Katherine, Doris, Helen, Mary

Helen, Ron, and Harold

Nab Family at Cherry Creek House

Aunt Esther Schmidt and Rebecca on Memorial Day

Helen, Grandma Bauer and Rebecca on Memorial Day

The Nab Family on Christmas Eve

Uncle Charlie Schmidt, Harold, and Ron at a family dinner

Sugar beet harvest

Uncle Charlie Schmidt making German garlic sausage

Tim, Rebecca, and my beloved 3 legged dog Tramp

Grandpa John Nab's Cottage

The Circle

ON MARCH 17, 2007, HAROLD, MY father, the man with the china blue eyes and melting smile passed through the veil. He did not want to go. He did not want to go for one reason only. He didn't want to leave "Helen Honey", my Mom, the grand passion of his life. He told me many times as he grew older that he loved her "more today than when I married her". He hung on to life longer than he should have and spent two years in a care center, but my mother was there every day of those last days. She put life on hold entirely, and devoted her days to Daddy. I think sometimes she wasn't aware of time passing or even what day it was. And finally, the little circle of our family was broken after sixty six years. Mother was exhausted and empty, and just plain tired.

Nikki and I begged, talked, and pleaded with her to come and spend Thanksgiving with us in Arizona. We had decided to show her the best time possible to reward her for her sacrifice for Dad. She finally said yes, and I flew to Denver to meet her plane and bring her home to my home. She stayed for twelve glorious days. We shopped at the finest stores; we went to a five star spa and had manicures and pedicures. We went to see the Rockettes put on their Christmas Show. We had lunch on the terrace of golf club overlooking the eleventh green on a sunny afternoon and sipped a glass of the finest pinot noir. And as I sat and looked at my tiny little china doll mother and my gloriously beautiful daughter, it occurred to me, "my goodness! We have come so far - far from the steppes of Russia – far from the poverty of the farm – far from being foreigners in a foreign land, and Nikki and I owed so much to my grandparents who braved the journey nearly half way around the world, but especially to Helen, my mother, who had one foot in Russia, and one foot in America, and sacrificed all for us to be Americans, and educated, and successful. At eighty five, she was having her first sushi, her first crab puff, her first fine wine. It was her first time at a country club, and her first pedicure.

The circle has been broken, but it is mending, and those of us here will carry on and do great things to thank all our Volga Deutsch ancestors for giving us strength, fortitude, and best of all – wonderful food and recipes that keep bringing us together to share and enjoy.

Thank you to my crazy wonderful family for living the stories so that I could write them.

Farewell

WHEN MY GRANDPARENTS LEFT RUSSIA, THINGS were very bad with the Bolshevicks overrunning the steppes and the villages, taking everything from the Volga Germans, even hanging the men and raping the women. And, of course, conditions only got worse. For the Wolgadeutsh, leaving Russia, however, there was a sadness about losing their way of life, their families left behind, their farms, their country. As the people crossed over the borders of Russia, they took a handful of soil with them and sang this farewell melody.

"At the borders of Russia

We will fill our hands with earth

And kiss it with thankfulness

For giving us care, food, and drink,

You dear dear Fatherland."

Henry Bauer   Margaret Adams Bauer   Katherine Adams

Terms and Definitions

Au gratin	Topped with crumbs and/or grated cheese and browned in the oven or under the broiler.
Au jus	Served in its own juice (particularly when speaking of beef).
Baste	To pour or spoon pan drippings, marinade, or cooking juices over meats while cooking to prevent drying out and to add flavor.
Bisque	A thick cream soup.
Blanch	To immerse in rapidly boiling water and allow to cook slightly
Boil	To heat a liquid until large bubbles break out on the surface. The boiling temperature at sea level is 212 degrees. A rolling boil is simply a vigorous boil. The boiling point is reached when a liquid is heated just until it begins to form bubbles.
Bone	To remove the bones from meat, poultry, or fish to debone.
Braise	To brown meat, lightly coated in flour, over high heat in a small amount of fat, or under the broiler, and then to simmer it in seasoned liquids in a covered pot.
Bread	To cover with fine dry bread crumbs before cooking.
Cream	To soften a fat, especially butter, by beating it at room temperature. Butter and flour or butter and sugar are often creamed together, to make a smooth soft paste.
Crimp	To seal the edges of a two-crust pie either by

pinching them at intervals with the fingers or by pressing them together with the tines of a fork.

Crudités An assortment of raw vegetables served as an hors d'oeuvre and often accompanied by a dip.

Cube To cut into cubes ½ -inch on a side or larger.

Curdle To clot or coagulate (particularly when speaking of milk, cream, and such sauces as cream sauces or hollandaise).

Cut in To combine solid fats and dry ingredients, especially shortening and flour, by chopping with two knives or with a pastry blender.

Degrease To remove fat from the surface of stews, soups, or stock. Usually, the latter is allowed to cool in the refrigerator, so that fat hardens and is easily removed.

Dice To cut into cubes less than ½ -inch in size.

Dredge To coat lightly with flour, cornmeal, and so on.

Drippings Juices and browned particles that collect in the bottom of the pan in which meat or poultry has been roasted; used to enrich and flavor sauces and gravies.

Entrée The main course.

Fillet To debone meat or fish. A fillet is the resulting tenderloin of beef or piece of fish without bones.

Flake To separate into small pieces in the direction of the grain; used particularly when speaking of fish.

Fold To incorporate a delicate substance, such as whipped cream or beaten egg whites, into another substance without releasing air bubbles. A spatula is used to gently bring part of the mixture from the bottom of the bowl to the top; the process is repeated, while slowly rotating the bowl, until the ingredients are thoroughly blended.

Fry :

Pan-fry To cook food in hot oil or fat, usually over direct heat. The food is not stirred, but is simply cooked on one or both sides.

Deep-fat fry To cook food by immersing it completely in heated fat.

Stir-fry A Chinese method of preparing meat or vegetables by cooking very rapidly in a frying pan or wok over very high heat, stirring constantly.

Glaze To cover with a glossy coating, either a concentrated stock for meats or a melted and somewhat diluted jelly for fruit desserts.

Julienne To cut meats, vegetables, fruits, or cheeses into match-shaped slivers.

Marinade Usually a strong flavored liquid, cooked or uncooked, used to make meats tastier and more tender; typically made of wine, olive oil, or a combination of the two, and seasoned with carrots, onion, bay leaf, and other herbs and spices. Other popular marinades are based on soy sauce and lemon juice. A dry marinade is a combination of herbs and spices, rubbed into meat, which is then allowed to stand before cooking. To marinate is to let food stand in marinade, either at room temperature or in the refrigerator, before cooking. Most recipes specify the length of time to marinate; recipes can vary from ½ hour to overnight to a couple of days.

Mince To chop into very small pieces.

Parboil	To boil until partially cooked. Usually this procedure is followed by final cooking in a seasoned sauce.
Pare	To remove the outermost skin of a fruit or vegetable.
Plump	To soak dried fruit, most often raisins, in warm water before cooking or adding to batter.
Poach	To cook very gently in hot liquid kept just below the boiling point.
Puree	To mash food perfectly smooth by hand, by rubbing through a sieve or food mill, or by whirling in a blender or food processor.
Reduce	To boil down a liquid until the quantity has decreased to about half of its original volume; its flavor becomes more concentrated.
Refresh	To run cold water over food that has been parboiled, to stop the cooking process quickly.
Render	To obtain fat from small pieces of meat by heating until it melts.
Roux	Pronounced roo, this is a mixture of flour and butter used as the base for a sauce. White roux is cooked briefly without browning (to make sure that the sauce will not have a raw-flour flavor); for a brown roux, the flour-butter mixture is allowed to brown evenly before the liquid is added.
Sauté	To cook and/or brown food in a small quantity of very hot fat, stirring or turning frequently.
Scald	To heat just below the boiling point, when tiny bubbles appear at the edge of the saucepan.
Sear	To brown and seal the surface of meat quickly, in a very hot oven or in a frying pan, over high heat.
Simmer	To cook in liquid just below the boiling point. The

surface of the liquid should be barely moving, broken from time to time by slowly rising bubbles.

Steep   To let food stand in hot liquid to extract or to enhance flavor, such as tea in hot water or poached fruits in sugar syrup.

Toss   To combine ingredients gently with a lifting motion.